Creating
your own
work

Creating your own work

WRITTEN AND IILLUSTRATED

BY

Micheline Mason

Gresham Books

© Micheline Mason 1980

First limited edition by GLAID 1978

Second edition 1980

Gresham Books
The Gresham Press
Old Woking
Surrey

ISBN 0 905418 80 8

*Shell U.K. Limited point out that the opinions expressed
by the author in this book are purely personal and not
necessarily to be regarded as views of Shell U.K. Limited.*

Jacket design by Eric Evans

Typeset by Reproprint, Leatherhead, Surrey
Printed by Unwin Brothers Limited,
Old Woking, Surrey.

Many thanks to:

Lionel and Ann Barnard, Robert Bowell, Tim Appleyard, Mary Underwood, Martin of 'Mitchell & Malick', Rosemary Carter, Stewart and Dave of 'Goldford Furnishings', 'Little Women', Jean Davies, Michael and Heather Ackland, Sue and Tim Currant, Anne Hoffman, Mailie Dans-Fleur, Dorothy Atree, Mrs Tolfree and Eleanor Tolfree, Helen and Richard Vine, Mary Potter, Libby Calvert, A. J. Martin, Heldey Holgate, Rod Ward, A. P. Woolrich, John Flack, Paul Stone — for their personal contributions; Pat Kitto and Stan and Lorna Windass for Board and Lodging; Ann and Kenneth Clark for encouragement and much information; Diana De Jonk for typing the final copy; Sue Moody for careful reading and editing, and the many other friends who helped to keep my nose to the grindstone.

Micheline.

Whilst every attempt has been made to be factually accurate with the information in this book, I would be grateful to be advised of any ommission or inaccuracies to assist with the preparation of the next edition.

—oOo—

CONTENTS

INTRODUCTION

'Then a ploughman said, Speak to us of work. And he answered saying: You work that you may keep pace with the earth and the soul of the earth. For to be idle is to become a stranger unto the seasons, and to step out of life's procession that marches in majesty and proud submission towards the infinite.

When you work you are a flute through whose heart the whispering of the hours turns to music.

Which of you would be a reed, dumb and silent, when all else sings together in unison....

.... Work is love made visible.

And if you cannot work with love but only distaste, it is better that you should leave your work and sit at the gate of the temple and take alms of those who work with joy.

For if you bake bread with indifference, you bake a bitter bread that feeds but half of man's hunger.

And if you grudge the crushing of the grapes, your grudge distils a poison in the wine....'

from 'The Prophet' Kahlil Gibran.

Kahlil Gibran's words offer a direct challenge to the present day understanding of the word 'work'. Most people grow up expecting to have a job which is reasonably well paid, useful, and fairly satisfying. We are told that if we work hard at school, perhaps doing well enough to go to college or even university, then we will have the opportunity for better paid jobs, for greater satisfaction and higher esteem than if we idle away our hours staring out of windows or playing football.

Leaving school however can bring one face to face with a harsh world that does not seem interested in what happened in 1066. A world where jobs are becoming more and more scarce, and their purposes more obscure. Consequently, one's future which once seemed so colourful and secure turns out to be disappointing. It can be a struggle to find a job, and an even greater struggle to find one which satisfies, challenges or fulfills in any way. However, as our financial commitments grow, so we compromise our desire to enjoy work with our need to have money. Today, many people are unable to find a job at all, let alone have a choice of work and so they join the growing numbers of unemployed. These problems face all Western industrially advanced societies yet none has agreed on a cause, or solution. Many societies are still burying their heads in the sand, hoping that unemployment is a temporary problem caused by a 'world recession', and that it will soon go away. In our

3

braver moments, however, most of us will admit to a deep-seated suspicion that the problem is not going to get better, but worse.

But one of the wonderful things about human nature is that when we are finally forced to face a problem head-on, sometimes we learn from it, and, occasionally, we even use the problem as a springboard to a new understanding, and a new creative response. There is nothing like being unemployed to make one question the meaning and purpose of work. Kahlil Gibran's writings with their direct challenge to the present day understanding of the word 'work', have touched many hearts even in today's cynical atmosphere.

Do we not all, deep down, believe that we were made to work, and to work purposefully? Do we not derive a great satisfaction from being effective and appreciated for the things we do? And do we not also know that work done with 'distaste' helps little, and embitters the one working? And what of our definitions of the word 'work', and the value judgements we put on it in terms of financial reward and prestige? How does this affect our ability to enjoy and feel fulfilled at unpaid work such as motherhood, which we may still feel is more 'real' than many forms of paid work which are 'contrived'?

How does it affect us when we know that our status and considered 'success' is measured by our income and visible material possessions, especially if we know we are only happy whilst weaving tapestries, at which we could barely scrape a living?

It takes a special clarity of vision and determination to break free from the enormous weight of these social attitudes, prejudices and fears, not to mention the practical limitations and demands these attitudes place upon us, and to create for ourselves a working space and pattern tailor-made to suit our individual needs and talents, aspirations and limitations. But it can be done, and is being done every day.

What makes us feel it will be so difficult? In Britain our particular attempt to balance our policies between socialism and capitalism seems to have created a certain half-heartedness within people. We do not wish to renounce our democracy and freedom in favour of total socialism in which the motivation to work is (theoretically at least) selfless, but nor do we seem too keen to put our hearts and souls into the competitive every-man-for-himself philosophy that pure capitalism demands. Instead, we hover between the two, feeling a little confused, somehow overwhelmed by the complications and size of the problems, and feeling powerless to change anything. Powerlessness breeds insecurity, but, like an overprotected child who becomes insecure, we are often not aware that our essential strengths have been weakened and deprived of challenge and encouragement. The insecurity often makes us look outside of ourselves for protection and answers, or for a scapegoat to blame when things go wrong.

The problem of insecurity has an answer, but an answer that takes a great deal of courage to realise, and demands the inate flexibility of the human

4

intelligence. The movement in the last few years towards self-help, self-sufficiency and a new awareness of the problems of size and centralisation, has essentially been led by a few people who wanted to reclaim the responsibility for their lives and those of their fellows, as well as responsibility for their environment. They wanted to reclaim their basic skills and powers of self-expression and to give free rein to their initiative. They have questioned and challenged our value-system, and begun to fight for the liberation of all those including women, black people and people with disabilities who have been oppressed by the false values under which we have lived. These people have taken the first few halting steps towards a new kind of society in which technology is used to fulfil real human needs, and not solely material needs.

This book is aimed at people who are hesitating before making an attempt to create their own work, and at those who have recently started, perhaps only just realising how much there is to learn. I have tried to amass a broad selection of information into a readable whole, none of which is heavily detailed, but most of which leads to sources of further information, if that is required. Included are both conventional techniques and sources of advice and assistance for would-be entrepreneurs, and a sprinkle of alternative-style projects and thinking which are blossoming like flowers on a rubbish tip. To bring the 'grit' alive and, more importantly, to give it all credibility, it is interspersed with pictures and illustrated with stories of people who deserve all our praise for paving the way for us by taking brave initiatives in the field of self-created employment.

Chapter One

The First Step

or whatever made me do it?

CHAPTER ONE: Motivation

The first Step, or Whatever made me do it?

The variety of motives offered to me for starting their ventures were as numerous as the people I met. However, they did fall into three main categories, each with their own different considerations – those who chose to; those who had to; and those who fell into it while they weren't looking!

Lionel and Ann Barnard

Of those who chose to, Lionel and Ann Barnard gave a clear description of the sequence of events and decisions they made before finally taking the plunge.

They are a married couple, who originally both worked for the same firm, Ann as a secretary, Lionel as an accountant. Their decision to change direction in their working lives sprang from a desire to obtain more personal freedom and satisfaction from their labours. They felt trapped in a consumer pattern of behaviour of accumulating more and more wealth, property, prestige and all its trappings, whilst having less and less time to enjoy it. Their decision to work for themselves was implemented slowly and carefully. Their first move was to cut down their outgoing expenditure by eliminating all they didn't really need. They sold their big home in Brighton and bought a small one in Henfield. They sold their large car in favour of a small one, and so on, until they had worked out the minimum income upon which they were prepared to live. While they were both still employed, they experimented with making hand-made toys, something they both felt they would enjoy doing, although it was a field in which neither had any previous experience.

They made dolls' houses, advertising one in the local newspaper, which brought in thirty replies. Ann began to make miniature peg dolls and furniture with which to stock the houses. As Lionel and Ann's skills and imagination developed, the range grew to include model shops stocked with exquisite hand-made miniature plaited raffia hats on wooden hat stands; wickerwork baskets, individually modelled, and painted clay vegetables in crates, sacks of potatoes, meat pies and many more. Miscellaneous items for collectors included a tiny woven basket inside which were two wooden knitting needles, and four balls of wool, and a piece of knitting in progress; the whole item measured about $1\frac{1}{2}$" in diameter.

When the couple felt secure in the knowledge that they could earn, through the regular sale of their toys, the minimum income previously estimated, they left work to become full-time toy-makers. The total transition took about eighteen months. Lionel and Ann were not people who would have been happy taking a loan to launch their business, so they deliberately chose something

8

which did not involve much capital outlay to start with. They had a few tools lying about the house, and as they built up their business, they gradually increased their stock of equipment. In addition to this, because they are both self-employed and therefore do not get paid in times of illness and other mishaps, they have built up a stock of household 'special offers' from supermarkets and grocery stores. Their cupboards are overflowing with tubes of toothpaste, tins of beans and other essential items.

They sell most of their toys through shops. They joined The British Toymakers' Guild (see chapter 8), who approved their designs, and advised on costing, marketing, suppliers of raw materials, and by putting members in touch with one another.

This couple exude an aura of calm to be envied by many an ulcer-chasing businessman. They seem totally contented with each other's company and say they have no wish to expand as they have set their sights where they wanted them.

Robert Bowell

Many professions can be adapted to be practised from home and for people with active minds but limited physical abilities, this can sometimes be an ideal way to work.

Robert Bowell suffers from a severe congenital disability which means he has a fine brain but very little brawn. It is very unlikely that he would have ever found outside employment, but the imagination with which he was born has driven him to make use of all the inner and outer resources available to him so enabling him to work. He is an Accountant.

When I entered his office, I realized that while advanced technology has caused many problems, for some people it has meant a new lease of life. The room was full of electronics. Robert greeted me warmly from his electric wheelchair, operated by a sucking tube. On the front of his desk is a switch which, when depressed, operates his Possum Unit. 'Possum' in Latin means 'to be able' and is the name given to electronic units which can control electrical apparatus by as little movement as the wink of an eye. Up on the wall was a box which was divided into two vertical panels. Each panel was subdivided into sections labelled 'radio', 'telephone', 'door', or 'alarm'. As Robert pressed the lever on his desk, a light clicked continuously from one section to the next until he let go of the lever, at which point the light stopped and the appropriate apparatus began to operate, i.e. the radio came on, or the door opened. By skilful operation, one could have both the radio and door operating at the same time, and if one were in a particularly mischievous mood, one could have the radio blaring, alarms ringing, lights flashing, doors opening and closing, whilst simultaneously typing a message on the typewriter and speaking on the telephone. As you have probably guessed, however, this is not the purpose for which it was intended! It was installed by Possum, and paid for by the 'Employment Service Agency' as an aid to Employment. Any electrical appliance can be attached to the Possum Unit. Robert, for example, connects it to a calculator, electric typewriter and the telephone.

Robert took O level Maths, English and History, and then A level Maths at home with an amanuensis. He decided to develop his liking and talent for figures into a career and arranged to have three years tuition at home in Book-Keeping, Income Tax Law and Practice, and Accountancy, taking the Royal Society of Arts Examination at home. At this time he had none of the equipment described above, which was obviously vital to enable him to set himself up in the business. The Government at first refused him a grant with which to buy the special controls until he could prove that he had a 'viable income'. How was he to secure a viable income without the means to do it? Luckily the Possum Users Association, a charity run entirely by users of Possum equipment, has a store of equipment to loan members. Thus, with borrowed equipment, Robert advertised his services in the local newspaper. When clients rang, he explained that they would have to come to him. The number of clients grew slowly, and at the beginning were often cases which were not easy to deal with. Now, however, he has enough work to use two assistants, one of whom is also self-employed, suffering from multiple sclerosis. The other (who is able bodied) helps from time to time doing some book-keeping and extracting figures for VAT returns as, with businesses such as Public Houses, this is more than either Robert or his colleague can manage.

After involving their MP, the battle with the Manpower Services Commission has been won and they have bought him the equipment he needs under their Business on Own Account Scheme. Robert's life looks like getting better and busier. Not only does he have several voluntary responsibilities, an increasing number of visits from clients, but the day before my visit, he had just announced to his somewhat stunned parents, that while they had been on holiday, he had fallen in love with his nurse and that they were soon to be married.

Tim Appleyard

Of those who started off on a path thinking it led nowhere much, and discovered that it led to a new way of life, Tim Appleyard must surely be a supreme example.

He is a married man with two young children, and is by profession a Maths and Science Teacher.

About five years ago he tried to raise some money for the Church Restoration Fund by 'scratching some rotten designs' on some cheap, plain glasses, intending to put them on a stall at the fund-raising Fete. In order first to get a little reassurance that the glasses were good enough to sell to the public, he showed a few people his efforts, and, to his astonishment, landed himself with £60 worth of orders.

The original designs were executed with a power 'Burgess' engraving tool, but Tim soon found this to be too clumsy and began to fashion his own tools with diamond chips, donated by a friendly jeweller, set into the shafts of felt-tip pens with jewellers' shellac.

These tools were like fine pencils, and drew white lines on the glass. With these he painstakingly copied photographs of birds, butterflies, animals, and buildings, or whatever the customer wished. Sometimes he tested the designs first on scraper board, for which the technique and results are similar.

Satisfied customers led to further orders, and he found more and more of his spare time was taken up by glass engraving. Buying uncut glass became a problem as it has to be bought direct from glass factories who often take months to fulfil an order. To cope with this, Tim has invested in a stock of uncut glass for use by himself and other engravers, for whom he runs a mail order service.

When he began, glass engraving was a rare hobby, but now the Guild of Glass Engravers has been formed, adding to Tim's life the company and support of other engravers as well as their constructive criticism. CoSIRA (see Chapter 8) have also helped by advice and exhibiting his work in their local Crafts Exhibition.

As his skill and technique have improved with practice, his hobby has become progressively more profitable, and when I visited him, he was completing his last term as a teacher, with the intention of becoming a full-time engraver. His solicitor was progressing with plans to make Tim's enterprise into a company, bringing the advantage of limited liability (see Chapter 3) and the benefit of reduced wholesale prices of glass. He was planning also to build a workshop out in the garden, as an alternative to the bedroom and loft which were then his working space.

'One of the myths' he said 'of working at home, is that you become isolated. When you go out, you may see people, but you do not really meet them.' On the day I visited, a Sunday, I was the second 'business' visitor, and a third was expected in the evening.

Tim's advice to would-be engravers is to go out and see what other engravers are doing, and then go home and try to reproduce it, even on old bottles. You will be delighted to know that once you have mastered the bottle, the better quality glass you use, the easier it will become.

What have they got that I haven't?

The key factor that separates those who have a go from those who don't, seems to be not talent, nor an innovative idea, nor pots of money, nor in fact, any special advantage, but perseverance, and the ability to enjoy the chosen work. There is no point at all in taking up a craft or profession which you find tedious or boring, because it is unlikely that you will have the involvement or

11

motivation to reach a high standard, or the endurance to carry the business through its early days which are always the hardest.

Many people began slowly, building up their confidence as small successes piled up. It is important, if you are contemplating jumping in at the deep end, that you are prepared for failure as well as success. If you feel you would be devastated, then perhaps it would be wiser to go to the other end of the pool and walk down the steps one by one.

What is success?

When exploring motivation do not forget to define success in your own terms. While for some, success means a certain level of income, or as high an income as possible, for others this is not so.

One couple I visited were extremely reluctant to have any publicity in case more people came to pressurise them with orders. They would only speak to me if I promised not to publish their names or addresses; but having given them my word, they were pleased to talk about, and display their work. They ran a small pottery, making individually thrown 'Pots for the People', which they sold in their small shop. Their delight was to earn a modest income whilst having the time to create special pieces and ceramic models, such as an individually commissioned chess-set. Their shop had a shelf full of pieces with which they could not bear to part. Humpty Dumpty, Alice in Wonderland, and other creations stood 'for display only'. There was even a slight air of resentment when commissioned pieces were collected by their owners before the couple had had sufficient time to enjoy them.

Having made your own definition of success, do not let others, whose definitions may be different from yours, dissuade, pressurise, or sidetrack you into something else.

What is failure?

Schulz, the creator of Charlie Brown and all the other Peanuts characters, learnt to draw by a correspondence course, because he was too afraid to go to Art School. He has used his understanding of our human fears and shortcomings, to create a cartoon strip that owes its phenomenal success to the appeal it makes to the universal human condition — failure. Failure is something we all experience whilst feeling we are the only one. Somehow failure is not faced aloud, and therefore becomes a lonely secret. We feel that to be a failure is to be unlovable, unrespectable, different. Yet we all secretly sympathise with Charlie Brown when he sighs 'Oh boy, I can't even lose properly'. Perhaps we are all still smarting from the memories of school reports, and many people have no intention of taking risks with new ventures at which they are not certain of success, for fear of the world's ridicule, which they are sure will befall them should they not succeed.

Yet when a baby begins to walk, we expect her to fall down many times. We pick her up and comfort her, and set her on her feet again and encourage her every step until she wobbles around without falling. We do not expect the baby to pick up a spoon for the first time in her life and begin to tuck into her mashed prunes and bacon without spilling a drop, nor do we snatch away the spoon at the first dollop on the wall, and never let her try again. We ignore the dollops on the wall, and on her face, and those dripping down her pelican bib, and cheer the half a teaspoon that actually finds its way into her mouth. We do this instinctively, knowing that this is how baby learns to do things for herself. Well, this is how people of all ages learn to do things for themselves – by making mistakes. By instilling in young people the fear of making mistakes, we effectively stop them learning. I once went on a residential counselling course which was geared towards helping people to regain their self-confidence. To make a break from the intense mental work that was involved, volley ball had been put on the time-table, but volley ball with a difference. Every time you missed the ball, someone gave you a hug. This had a profound effect on most people who had been brought up with competitive games. Suddenly you can see failure in a new light, that it is no more than baby falling over or spilling her food. It is cruel to deny a person the right to make mistakes. Failure, in a permanent sense, can only belong to those who have been made so afraid to make mistakes that they never even try. If you try, even though your actual venture may possibly not work, you as a person, cannot be a failure. You will surely be a better and richer personality for the experience.

A Good Start is a Good Finish

Please look after this Bear

Chapter Two

Design

CHAPTER TWO: Design

A Good Start is a Good Finish

When contemplating a manufacturing or craft project, do not spend too long putting off your venture because you have not come up with a stunningly original design. I remember at Art College, one of the lecturers suddenly bellowing at a startled student 'Stop trying to develop a style of your own! You cannot *help* having a style of your own!' And it is true.

To design is to solve problems, so before the final product the solution can be reached: the problem must first be identified and defined. If design relates to an object then its purpose is of prime importance so one should try to achieve that purpose simply and economically. It may be fruitful to look at the way such problems have been solved historically, but the value of an individual design will rest in the special quality of the solution. Design can also refer to embellishment or decoration so for those with little experience of drawing or design it may be helpful to start by using simple geometric symbols and patterns and thereby explore the relationships of these elements in the particular context of the materials and techniques that you intend to use.

It is not recommended that you copy the designs of other contemporaries as you may be contravening Patent or copyright laws or indeed be accused of plagiarism.

Should you be interested in natural forms as a basis of designs, drawing from nature (whatever your standard of drawing) can be a sound source of inspiration. Visits to museums to study the ways that natural forms have been used in decoration can also be stimulating.

A visit to the Design Centre in London or the Scottish Design Centre in Glasgow can give a good idea of what are some of the best designs available and an indication of the standards with which you may be competing.

The Design Centre is at 28 Haymarket, London, SW1 and the Scottish Design Centre at 72 Vincent Street, Glasgow, C2.

Having decided on your final design and made a few prototypes, treat it with the respect it deserves. Several people I met spoke warningly of a fate which had befallen them as a result of being too trusting with their treasured designs. They had taken the prototypes proudly to a store-buyer, hopefully to obtain orders, only to be disappointed a few days later by the return of the samples accompanied by a polite 'No thank you'. A few months later they saw the same designs on sale in the shop, almost direct copies. To protect a design which you believe to be original, you can do one of three things: patent, register, or copyright the design.

16

A Patent

If you have an invention where the novelty lies not so much in the appearance of the article, but in its construction, operation or function, you can write to HM Patent Office (Department of Trade and Industry), Southampton Buildings, Chancery Lane, London WC2, who will send you a leaflet entitled 'Applying for a Patent'. This tells you in great detail what to do, but advises that an application for a Patent must be accompanied by a 'specification', which is a specialised document both legal and technical. Unless you have experience in dealing with these documents, you are usually well advised to enlist the help of a registered Patent Agent. A list of Agents is published by the Chartered Institute of Patent Agents, Staple Inn Buildings, London WC1. Telephone 01 405 9450.

Registered Design

A design is defined as meaning 'Features of shape, configuration, pattern or ornament applied to an article by any industrial process or means, being features which in the finished article appeal to, and are judged solely by the eye, but does not include a method or principle of construction or features of shape or configuration which are dictated by the function which the article to be made in that shape or configuration has to perform'. Therefore, design in this sense has to do with appearance and not with function or fabric. Application for protection of a design is also made through the Patent Office. It may happen that your article may require both patenting its novel functioning features, and registration of the unique design with which it has been decorated.

Beware of the idea-stealers incognito, and try to keep your design a secret until you have sneaked down to the Patent Office.

Copyright

Copyright is a form of protection available to artists and writers, which allows them to prevent others from copying their work. Copyright covers the whole field of literature and the crafts, including books, articles, poems, paintings, photographs, music, sculpture and other forms of artistic creation.

Copyright law is quite complex, but basically it states that the copyright for any artistic creation belongs automatically to the artist, unless affected by a written or verbal agreement with another party. Sometimes, for example, if you are commissioned to do work for someone else, the copyright may belong to the client along with the commissioned designs. Similarly a designer working for a salary may forfeit his copyright rights to his employer. It is wise before starting work to come to an agreement over these matters, and also to specify what you are paid to do.

The law prevents others from knowingly making a direct copy of an artist's work, but cannot prevent artists, or writers simultaneously creating and publishing identical pieces of work independently of each other.

Finishing

Almost as important as the design is the careful making and finishing of your work. Sandpaper all the rough bits, darn in all the ends, polish it until you see your exhausted reflection. If the finishing means investing in machines to help you along and to speed up the process, then take the risk of investing in them. This attention to detail often makes the difference between production as a hobby, and production to earn a living.

Mary Underwood

Mary Underwood was not making much progress in her project of making Paperweights from Polyester Resin until her husband made for her two small machines from old washing-machine motors – a lapping wheel and polishing mops.

The paperweights are made in moulds – stainless steel sundae dishes – with flowers and dried grasses embedded in the clear plastic. Mary's speciality is embedding perfectly intact dandelion puffs.

When they come out of the moulds, the paperweights are of the standard reached by many amateur 'plasti-craft' hobbyists, but when ground and polished by Mary's equipment, they make a handsome glass-like ornament which she can sell easily at craft shops and art galleries. Her craft started in the kitchen, but unfortunately the distinctive smell of the resin affected the taste of all the food that was prepared there, and the family, fed up with resin-flavoured meals, persuaded her to move to another small room in which the odour could be trapped. Apart from natural materials, Mary embeds taken-apart watches, and indeed will take orders to embed any precious object including medals. Selling these paperweights is no problem. Mary knows she cannot make as many as she could sell.

In addition to the paperweights, Mary makes Hessian Character Dolls, a craft she learnt entirely from books. She makes Hessian Druids and Monks, Bishops and Tweedy Ladies, as well as the old faithful, Paddington Bear.

Each doll has an accessory such as a Bible, or a rush basket, some knitting, or a clinging child. Her daughter Judith helps her with the cutting-out and machining of these dolls, and they are sold alongside the paperweights.

These two crafts give Mary the variety and scope for her talents, which she desires.

Materials

If you are not sure where to find wholesalers and suppliers of suitable materials for your chosen product, Kompass Publications Limited (Stuart House, 41-43 Perrymount Road, Haywards Heath, Sussex) publish a directory called 'Kompass' which can be found in most reference libraries. It lists a huge range of commodities followed by long lists of suppliers which are marked by symbols to show, for example, if they are wholesalers or retailers. But this should not deter you from attempting your own ideas as practice is essential for attaining a standard of workmanship that makes a product commercially viable. It is not always easy to assess the quality of your own work, so do not be afraid to seek the advice and criticism of someone whose judgment you respect.

A single person or even a small group of people can never compete with mass production, so never try to make things that could just as easily (and possibly more cheaply) be manufactured industrially. Quality and individuality of design are where the small producer can excel.

Supposing I can't Dream Up a New Design?

LICENCE

If After racking your brains for ages, you are still unable to come up with any ideas as to what you would like to make, or which service you would like to provide, it is possible to 'licence' innovative ideas which have been chosen by the National Research and Development Corporation, as being worthy of further development. For more information about this see Chapter 7 (Financial Assistance).

FRANCHISE

There is, finally, the possibility of obtaining a franchise. A franchise is a contract which entitles you to trade under the name of an established organisation (such as 'Wimpey'). Whilst you are responsible for the everyday running of your 'branch', the central organisation remains responsible for such common services as supply of materials and publicity campaigns. Advice on obtaining a franchise can be obtained from: The Franchise Advisory Centre, 32 Stockwell Park Crescent, London SW9.

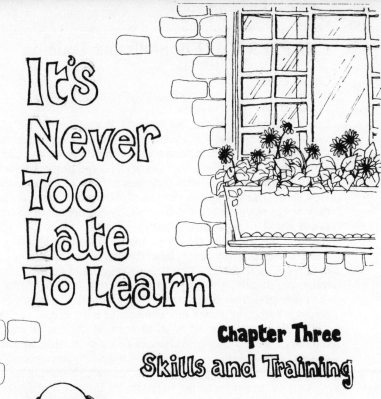

It's Never Too Late To Learn

Chapter Three
Skills and Training

CHAPTER THREE: Skills and Training

Its Never too Late to Learn

One of the effects of the last war still looked upon with nostalgia, was the sudden need for everyone, skilled or unskilled, male or female, fit or disabled, to work. People were expected to contribute their energies to all kinds of employment for the benefit of the whole community. Under these emergency conditions people found that they were capable of learning and practising in a very short time a whole variety of skills which under normal circumstances, they would not have had the opportunity nor dreamt of having the confidence to attempt. This capability to learn new skills is still within all of us, no matter what our age, yet, with the increasing trend towards specialisation in industry and commerce, many people label themselves as 'fitters', or 'packers', 'typists' or 'clerks', as if this is a complete description of their range of abilities, and, more importantly, a description of the limit, both now and in the future, of their potential. This is nonsense. The opportunity to learn new skills is, in this country, becoming wider and available to more people all the time.

The easiest skill for all of us to learn, is the one in which we have most interest. If we are willing to create our own work, then we have the freedom to choose and develop our special interests. Consequently, the necessary requirement of learning our chosen skill well, should not be difficult, but fun.

Many of the people whom I met during the period of research for this book, had begun their venture by developing a new hobby through taking out library books and practising and practising.

Training can consist of studying for qualifications, or learning a new craft at college or as an apprentice, or on your own. It may mean brushing up on old skills, or it may mean research into traditional or contemporary techniques and materials.

Basic Skills
Adult Education (full-time)
PUBLICATIONS
To find out what is available, and where:

'The Year Book of Adult Education' is a directory of organisations and courses both in Britain and abroad. It is published by the National Institute of Adult Education, 35 Queen Anne Street, London W1 – 01.637 4241; and it is also available at the Scottish Institute of Adult Education, 57 Melville Street, Edinburgh – 031.226 7200.

If you have no intention of leaving Britain in order to learn a new skill then another book called 'The Directory of Further Education', published by

Hobson's Press (Cambridge) Ltd lists all full-time and part-time courses held at recognised educational centres throughout the UK. It can be found in most Reference Libraries. Look in the back of the book for the name of the subject in which you are interested, and then refer to the page number listed beside your chosen subject. When you have found the page it will tell you the names of all the centres which do courses in that subject. You then look in another part of the book for the actual address of the institute. Near the back of the book is a section called 'Second Chance' which lists colleges all over the British Isles which design courses especially for mature students. Many offer crêche, nursery or playgroup facilities. In some areas there are work preparation courses for the disadvantaged, including Burton upon Trent Technical College, Lichfield Street, Burton upon Trent, Staffs DE14 2NB, and Doncaster Institute of Higher Education, Waterdale, Doncaster, South Yorkshire DN1 3EX.

There are Youth Opportunies Programme Schemes for Unemployed School Leavers at many colleges including Newcastle under Lyme College of Further Education, Liverpool Road, Newcastle under Lyme, Staffs ST5 2DF. There are also some programmes for people with disabilities. One college which has these is Bournville College of Further Education, Bristol Road South, Birmingham B31 2AJ.

For information on full-time design courses in England, Scotland, Wales, and Northern Ireland, see the 'Directory of Design Courses in the UK', including vocational, degree and post graduate courses in ceramics, glass, jewellery and silversmithing, textiles, furniture, and other crafts. It is published by The Design Council, 28 Haymarket, London SW1 – 01.839 8000.

A diploma in Art & Design (Dip.A.D.) has now re-classified as a BA in Art & Design. 'Courses leading to the diploma in Art & Design' is available free from The Art & Design Admissions Registry, 16 Albian Place, Maidstone, Kent – 0622 673 255.

COURSES
Apart from Adult Education courses run by the Education Department there are many centres, particularly in the field of crafts, set up by private individuals or groups, who are teaching the skills they are using to earn their livings. Some of these are also residential communities bound together by common beliefs in the self-help movement. A few of these are described later under 'Short Courses'.

Dartington Hall   Dartington Hall Estate in Devon, is a unique experiment in trying to combine education, work, community and the Arts into a unified whole. The idea grew in the mind of one of its founders Leonard Elmhirst, whilst he was working in Bengal with the Indian poet and philosopher Robindranath Tagore. Tagore believed that the Western city-dwelling man lived in a fragmented world, having lost any sense of the underlying unity that binds all beings and things. He saw that the only opportunity to bring the

23

strands together again was to revitalise traditional communities which still retained traces of old values.

Leonard, and his new wife Dorothy, an heiress to a millionaire, shocked local inhabitants when in 1925 they began a project which, then, must have seemed so outlandish as to be almost incomprehensible. They planned to rejuvenate a corner of Devon, and to this end bought Dartington Hall and its surrounding estate where, through the Trust which they set up, they attempted to create a working community in which people could find scope for personal development and a sense of fulfilment, as well as earn a living.

The Estate was formed under the guidance of Leonard Elmhirst, who was trained as an agriculturalist and who brought to Devon many innovations such as soil surveys and artificial insemination, as well as one of Devon's first tractors.

In 1926 they started a co-educational progressive school which now has about 330 fee paying pupils, all of whom share in the government of the school. There is a minimum of rules and almost no coercion, the emphasis being on the freedom of the individual. Dartington created new employment by re-establishing old industries – textiles and cider making, a saw mill and joinery works, and later the famous Dartington Glass Works. A pottery training workshop has been opened at the new craft-based 'Cider Press'.

The Trust has also encouraged a programme of Adult Education, and, in 1976, with the help of a grant from the Manpower Services Commission, a work experience scheme for unemployed school leavers was launched, combining earning and learning through a series of attachments to a wide range of departments, thus beginning, as was always intended, to use the entire estate and all its activities as an educational resource.

During the 1930s Dartington gained an international reputation in the Arts with well known painters, potters and theatre directors in residence. Since the last war, a college of Arts has developed which provides courses in Theatre, Music, Art and Design. The teaching is based on the idea that the value of Art lies not in its aesthetic value, but in the benefit derived from it by the whole community.

The Prospectus is available from the Admissions Secretary, Dartington College of Arts, Dartington, Totnes, Devon. Details of the Summer School of Music from the Registrar, Summer School of Music, 48 Ridgeway, Wimbledon, SW19.

Tops   If you take a full time course at an Adult Education Centre or college of further education you might be eligible for allowances under the Training Opportunities Scheme.

It is a public service operated by the Manpower Services Commission to help people improve their job prospects. If you are over 19 and have been away from full-time education for at least three years, then this scheme may help you. There are over 60 courses, and self-employed people are eligible, providing that they are not in business (earning) at the time. The big advantage of a Tops Course is that you are paid while you train. In addition to free training you will get:

(1) A weekly tax free allowance
(2) Free credits of National Insurance contributions
(3) A lodging allowance if you have to stay away from home
(4) Free midday meals or an allowance if they are not provided
(5) Your fare if you have to travel more than two miles for training

You may also be entitled to an earnings related supplement. Write to your local Employment Service Agency or Job Centre for details.

Adult Education (Part-time)

PUBLICATIONS
Your local Education Authorities will publish each year a full prospectus of all local part-time day and evening classes. If you can find several people who are interested in a particular subject, your local Education Department will attempt to provide you with a suitable instructor and to sponsor him/her to teach a class. Many local authorities make their classes available free of charge to people living on supplementary benefits.

If you live in London there is an excellent publication called 'Floodlight' which can be bought at newsagents and booksellers as well as being found at your local library. It lists the numerous part-time day and evening classes held within Inner London

COURSES
Correspondence Courses The advantage of correspondence courses is that you can fit your studying time to your other commitments with very little pressure. The Association of British Correspondence Colleges, 4 Chiswell St, London EC1 represents over 20 colleges which arrange courses covering subjects as far apart as arithmetic to zoology, at levels ranging from preliminary courses for complete beginners, to higher degree courses. Write to them for information, or ring 01.606 0255.

The Rapid Results College, Department DK4, Tuition House, London SW19 4DS is one of the many schools which arrange homework correspondence courses in subjects such as accountancy, book-keeping, computer studies & programming, and indexing.

Not all correspondence courses are academic. Courses for practical subjects can often be found advertised in appropriate magazines. Examples of non-academic courses include:

THE BRITISH HOROLOGICAL INSTITUTE, Upton Hall, Newark, Notts, 0636 81 3795, offering correspondence courses in horology.

THE FACILITY OF ASTROLOGICAL STUDIES, Hook Cottage, Vine Cross, Heathfield, Sussex, runs correspondence courses in Astrology.

THE ST NICHOLAS TRAINING COLLEGE, in Queensgate, London, runs a correspondence course in teaching by the Montessori method, although this course includes a Summer School for practical work in London which must be attended.

THE PREPARATORY TRAINING BUREAU is a unit of the Royal Association for Disability And Rehabilitation, (RADAR), 25 Mortimer St, London WIN 8AB. Their role is to prepare people who have had to undergo prolonged hospital treatment, or who, after the onset of an illness or disability are confined to their homes and need to be re-trained in a field of work that is appropriate to their new situation. RADAR runs correspondence courses which although sometimes specially written to particular educational needs, are usually channelled through normal correspondence schools. In a case where an applicant cannot afford to pay for a course himself, RADAR will arrange for him to receive a grant.

Short and/or Part-Time Courses   Of the many short and/or part-time courses available, here is a tiny selection to whet your appetite:

HOME MACHINE KNITTING (FOR COTTAGE INDUSTRIES) Preston Technical College, Corporation Street, Preston, Lancs PR1 2TQ.
Mabel Fletcher Technical College, Sandown Road, Liverpool L15 4JB.
Wigan College of Technology, Parsons Walk, Wigan, Lancs WN1 1RR.

WROUGHT IRON WORK, Welding, Furniture and Antique Furniture Restoration, Reinforced Plastics, Saddlery and Leatherwork, Thatching, Vehicle Electronics, Woodworking Machinery.
CoSIRA, PO Box 717, 35 Camp Road, Wimbledon Common, London SW19 (see Chapter 8).

CABINET MAKING London College of Furniture, 41-7 Commercial Road, London E1 1LA (includes special courses for the deaf).

CHINA AND PORCELAIN RESTORATION Marylebone Institute, Quintin Kynaston School, Marlborough Hill, London NW8 0NL.

SHOES, LEATHERGOODS AND HANDBAGS (DESIGN AND MANUFACTURE) Cordwainers Technical College, Mare Street, London E8 3RE.

MUSICAL INSTRUMENT MAKING (INCLUDING REPAIR AND MAINTENANCE) The London College of Furniture, Department of Musical Technology, 41-7 Commercial Road, London E1 1LA.

POTTERY, PAINTING BATIK AND OTHER CRAFTS The Bevere Vivis Group, Bevere Knoll, Bevere, Worcester WR3 7RQ.

ACCOUNTANCY, SILVERSMITHING, JEWELLERY AND ENGRAVING City of London Polytechnic, Administrative Headquarters, 117 Houndsditch EC3A 7BU.

PAINTING, TAPESTRY, WEAVING, SPINNING AND OTHER TEXTILE CRAFTS John and Mary Lloyd Jones, Yr Hen Ysgol, Aberbanc, Llandyssal, Dyfed, Wales.

BATIK Southwark College, The Cut, London SE1 8LE.
Camden Institute, 87 Holmes Road, NW5 3AX.

EMBROIDERY Gawthorpe Hall, Nelson and Colne College, Padiham, Burnley, Lancashire.

APPLIQUE, PILLOW LACE, MACRAME, Quilting, Patchwork, Rug-making, Beading Embroidery
The Embroiderer's Guild, 73 Wimpole Street, London W1.

BEAUTY THERAPY/BODY MASSAGE Celestial School of Beauticians Training, 62 Marylebone Lane, 3rd Floor, London W1.

GLASS The Glasshouse, 27 Neal Street, London WC2.

JEWELLERY Jewellery Summer School, Norman Crant, Mill Wynd, Lundin Links, Fife, Scotland.

SILVERSMITHING, LAPIDIARY, METALWORK, ENAMELLING Craft O' Hans, The Old Mill, Nannerch Nr Mold, Clwyd.

WEAVING, SPINNING AND DYING The Association of Guilds of Weavers, Spinners and Dyers, 7 Ralston Street, London SW3.

BASKETRY Central London Institute, 6 Bolt Court, Fleet Street, EC4A 3DY.

CALLIGRAPHY Eltham Institute, Haimo Road, Eltham, London SE9 6DZ.

CREATIVE METAL WORK Clapham and Balham Institute, 6 Edgeley Road, London SW4 6EL.

DESIGN FOR EXPERIENCED AMATEURS (basic design)
Mary Ward Centre, 9 Tavistock Place, London WC1H 9SP.
Working Men's College, Crowndale Road, London NW1.
Chelsea and Westminster Institute, Marleborough School, Sloane Avenue, London SW3.

27

INTRODUCTION TO COUNSELLING Morely College, 61 Westminster Bridge Road, London SE1 7HT.

BECOMING SELF-EMPLOYED Addison Institute, Addison School, Addison Gardens, London W14 0DT.

THE DOVE CENTRE The Dove Centre, Crispin Hall, Street, Somerset, and at Butleigh, Nr Glastonbury, Somerset, is a part resident community of people making high quality craft products and offering part-time, full-time and holiday courses. At Street there is a shop, gallery, theatre workshop, print-making, painting, drawing and weaving workshops. At Butleigh there are pottery, stained glass and furniture workshops.

The Open University The Open University is unique. It exists primarily to make a degree available to people over 21 who, though capable of study at University level, cannot attend a University full-time and may not have the 'O' and 'A' levels required. Indeed, no paper qualifications at all are required.

There are four foundation courses of which a student must normally do two, usually one at a time. These are Humanities, Social Science, Technology and Mathematics. All courses are based on correspondence packages, with written assignments to be submitted by students. There is a compulsory residential Summer School. Additional help is given by radio and TV broadcasts alongside the written assignment. The University year runs from January to December and applications should be made from the Autumn one and a quarter years ahead of the time you wish to take a course (e.g. Autumn 1977 to begin January 1979). Copies of the prospectus and an application form can be obtained by writing your name and address on a postcard and sending it to the Open University, Admissions PO Box 48, Milton Keynes, Bucks MK7 6AB.

Quiet and discipline are needed. It is a good idea if you have never studied seriously, to take evening classes beforehand, in order to get into the way of studying, and to learn to develop your personal discipline.

Original Research and Experimentation For some people, training, in relation to setting up their particular initiative, is of such an individual nature that established educational programmes will not suffice. It can mean many hours of research in libraries, archives, or by picking the brains of others. It can mean experimenting in the creation of completely new techniques, designs, materials, services, or in the application of skills to new areas.

MITCHELL & MALICK, MARBLERS The revival of ancient crafts can run into a special problem – the materials once used are no longer available; sometimes, it is difficult to discover even what they were.

Martin is a young man who became interested in marbling whilst working for a publisher. The Marbling of end-papers for books dates back to 1121 in Japan where the art was called *Sumina Gashi* or 'floating ink'. Martin was intrigued by the method which involves large trays of liquid, upon the surface of which float moving patterns of colours, seeming to be alive and magically changing before your eyes. Suddenly the patterns are captured forever on a piece of paper, no two ever alike.

Whilst still employed designing book-jackets, he began research into the traditional methods which have died out, partly because the water-based inks, as opposed to the oil-based inks commercially used nowadays, are no longer made. He spent two years studying, experimenting and practising with the chemicals of inks, pigments and the liquid bath solution made from sea-weed. He first attempted marbling in the bath in his London flat, later progressing to a work-shop in the garage.

With a friend as a partner, they started probably the only business in Britain, marbling in the traditional way. They had many difficult times getting large orders of matching end-papers to actually match, as many factors including minor changes of temperature affect the movement of the inks, a dilemma not helped by panicking.

They now have a workshop and showroom in the Devizes Road, Wiltshire, where I met Martin and his wife. After sizing me up he decided I was not an industrial spy, and invited me into his sea side-smelling workshop to demonstrate his craft.

I sat on a bench, hopefully out of range as he flicked different coloured pigments onto the surface of the liquid base with large paint-brushes. He drew an instrument like a wide-toothed comb through the liquid, making a regular pattern in the floating colours, flicked a bit more, then lay a plain piece of paper carefully flat on the surface of the liquid. When he slowly lifted the paper, the colours had adhered in exactly the pattern they had formed whilst floating.

Martin is planning to develop the art of marbling on fabrics, wood, and leather, and hopes to move into the country where he can set up a workshop employing other people. He gives lectures and demonstrations of marbling to colleges and groups, and cannot help but infect you with his fascination for the ancient craft.

Supplementary Skills

When contemplating running your own business, it is as well to accept the fact that paper work cannot be avoided. Whilst many people keep this to a minimum by employing the services of an accountant, it can do nothing but good to learn how to write well-balanced letters, how to keep your filing straight, simple book-keeping and the keeping of records. It is essential to begin right from the start to keep track of stock, cost of materials, overheads, time taken to make products or perform services, and the selling prices, in order to have any clear idea of the financial viability of your venture. This creates the dividing line between a hobby and a business.

The Rose Pottery

To illustrate the difference between starting a hobby and starting a business, Rosemary Carter's initiative in the setting up of a small pottery in her own home makes a good example.

Rosemary left Art College at the age of 21 where she had trained in pottery and sculpture, crafts at which she said she was more keen than good. She is partially sighted and completely colour blind, a condition which for many would have led towards simple and non-creative work such as being a telephone switchboard operator. Rosemary, however, was determined to make use of her skills, and to this end invested a modest inheritance in a small kiln and potter's wheel with which she began to make pots. From the beginning she took a business-like attitude towards her work, numbering each piece she made and keeping a list in a note book of the number, what it was, the price and the date she sold it. Soon she had enough work to display on a stall at a church fete and from here she began to take orders, and to allow visitors to come to see her work which she showed in a tiny room at home. She began to advertise in the CoSIRA Hand Book of 'Craft Work Shops' in the Countryside, which sometimes brought tourists to her door. As the number of visitors grew, some asked for demonstrations and some for lessons, and Rosemary now earns money both from selling pottery and from running childrens' and adults' classes in her little studio. She includes in her classes mentally and physically disabled children, and has adapted one of her wheels to be used by a handicapped child. Her latest hobby, as opposed to her business, is riding her new bicycle, which, as she says, 'is not bad for someone who can hardly see'.

Basic Routine System

Generally speaking the clerical work involved in the successful running of any small business consists of a few constant necessities.

A RECORD OF ALL EXPENDITURE

The following items will be entered by you or your accountant in the expenditure column of your books, and will almost undoubtedly give you a horrible shock. The main two reasons for subjecting yourself to this traumatic experience are, firstly, to be able to rationally price your finished product or service and consequently decide whether it will be marketable, and secondly to stop the tax man guessing at your profits, which he will do unless you can prove otherwise.

The purchase of raw materials Duplicate order-books can be purchased from stationers, and copies of all orders, invoices and receipts should be kept on file.

When goods are received they should be checked off against the order form. when bills are paid, the appropriate invoice should be marked 'Paid' with the date and 'Cash' or cheque number. Every item should be included right down to paper-clips.

Payment of Overheads   In addition to your private account, it is wise to open a second account specifically for the business. You will consequently receive separate cheque and paying-in books, and separate bank statements including those of standing orders. From this account pay all overheads relevant to your business, including a proportion of your normal household overheads if you are working from home (see Tax Allowance).

Petty cash   A petty cash account should be kept independently of your main accounts, as this money is the easiest to lose track of and can mount up amazingly. From a stationers buy a Petty Cash Book, and a pad of Petty Cash slips. Every item bought from Petty Cash should be entered on a slip with its cost, date of purchase, and who bought it. If possible a receipt for the purchase should be stapled to the appropriate slip. In your Petty Cash Book make an entry under 'Income' on the day that you draw the cash cheque from your Business Account, stating the amount. At the end of the appointed time (a week), list all the entries on the slips in your Petty Cash Book under 'Expenditure', and add them together. The balance between this total and the original 'Income' should equal the amount of cash left in your petty cash box. A new cheque is made out for the amount spent, to bring the total held back to the original sum.

Post book   If substantial amounts of mail leave your work place, it is wise to keep a post book. An amount of stamps are bought, using if necessary a 'stamp order form' (available from the Post Office).

They are entered in your Post Book with the date of purchase. Each letter sent is listed with the date, to whom sent, and the value of the stamps used. Every now and again the book is balanced and a fresh stock of stamps bought.

INCOME

Income is usually a simpler affair to record.

Estimates and invoices   Duplicates of all estimates and invoices sent to customers should be kept together in a file. When payment is received, they should be marked 'Paid' with the date and if issued, a copy of your receipt should be attached. Not only will this give you a record of your overall income, but also of who still owes you money.

Paying-in   Apart from payments relating to estimates and orders, all casual income should be clearly described on your paying-in slip and added to your records. When your bank statement is received, mark off all the cheques entered on your paying-in slip to make sure none of them have bounced. Also verify that the cheques which you have paid out have been presented.

31

Chasing debts When making out a bill or invoice, terms of payments should be stated at the head. If the bill is not paid within the terms stated, then a reminder should be sent out. Should this have no effect, after a suitable time has elapsed, a letter should be sent to the customer requesting immediate payment. If this is to no avail, it is advisable to place outstanding debts in the hands of a solicitor or accountant. He will require full details of the work done, together with copies of all correspondence regarding the debt. He will then take the necessary action to recover the money, and will charge, by way of a fee, a small percentage of the sum recovered. An alternative method is to file a plaint at the local County Court which is not difficult, but time consuming. The clerk of the court will ask for a form to be filled in giving details. A small fee is payable, but is added to the amount of the debt and is charged to the debtor. If there is any dispute concerning the debt before the plaint is filed, full details must be given to the court, and if the debtor then wants to contest the action for recovery of the debt, then a court appearance is necessary. Generally speaking however, unless there is any cause for complaint, it will be found that a request for payment received from the County Court will have immediate results. Failing all this, written off debts should be carefully recorded as a charge or allowance against the profits of the Business.

TAX ALLOWANCES
You will be interested to know that the more expenses, outgoing and allowances you are able to claim, the lower your tax bill will be.
   A self-employed person can claim tax benefit on:
(1) all allowable expenses
(2) capital allowances for equipment, machinery, etc
(3) tax-saving opportunities at the start of the business
(4) employing your wife or making her a partner
(5) setting loss off against income on which you would otherwise pay tax.

Allowable expenses
(a) lost raw materials
(b) general running expenses e.g. rent, rates, heating, lighting, telephone, tools, special clothing, postage, stationery, accountants' fees, advertising
(c) use of home as an office; proportion of rent, rates, lighting, heating, cleaning and insurance
(d) wages, salaries and pensions of employees
(e) life insurance, employers share of employee's national insurance stamps, sometimes VAT. (see VAT)
(f) entertaining of overseas customers, gifts for advertising, gifts to employees, and gifts to you
(g) grants given to you
(h) business travel expenses including running costs of car
(i) business payments of interests on loans and overdrafts

(j) business insurance
(k) normal repairs and maintenance of business premises
(l) bad debts
(m) legal expenses except those for acquiring property
(n) fees paid to register trade marks and designs
(o) some subscriptions to magazines and trade unions
(p) hiring equipment and the interest part only of hire purchase charges.

Capital allowances Full capital allowances are for plant or machinery, including cars and vans, office equipment and fixtures and fittings bought exclusively for use in the business. For anything bought to be shared between business and private use, a proportion of the capital allowance is given.

Tax-saving opportunities at the start of the business At present, a first year allowance of the whole cost of the capital equipment, or asset, is given against profits for the accounting year in which you buy it. However, you can choose an alternative which can be more beneficial to the small business in the long term. This is a choice of accepting an allowance on only part, or even none, of the cost of the asset in the first year, the total of the remaining unclaimed allowance then being called its 'written-down value'. Each year after the first you can claim an allowance on 25% of this written-down value, called a 'written-down allowance'.

BOOK-KEEPING AND CASH FLOW
Book-keeping is simply a case of recording all financial outgoings on one hand, called 'Expenditure', and all sales or fees on the other, called 'Income'. The Income less the Expenditure equals your profit, and discovering this amount is the main purpose of the exercise. Your 'Books' will form the basis for you or your Accountant from which to write up your Annual Accounts for the Tax Man.

Now, your balance at the Bank, plus the amount you are owed, less the amount you yourself owe, will give you an idea of what fresh expenditure you can risk making. This activity is called 'looking after your cash flow' and is vitally important. Not paying proper attention to your cash flow can lead to a chilly fate that has struck not only tiny ventures struggling for survival, but also rapidly growing and healthy looking firms. Simply, one spends sums of money to buy materials to meet a fat order book, but the suppliers of these materials want their cash faster than the customers orders can be completed and paid for. Having invested your capital in the premises, tools and machinery and materials necessary to do the work, there is just not enough ready cash to pay your bills. This unhappy situation can, and often does lead to sitting miserably before a row of stony-faced creditors who have the legal powers to liquidate a small business. If you are not a Company with Limited Liability (see Chapter 3) you may also find to your horror that you can be ordered to sell your private possessions in order to pay your debts.

33

AUDITED ACCOUNTS

You are obliged by law to have your accounts audited by a Chartered Accountant if you are a Limited Company, Charity or Co-operative. The Auditor will issue you with an official Balance Sheet and Profit and Loss Account for the previous year. Accountants can be found in the yellow pages or by recommendation.

STOCK

All items of stock should be listed under headings of description, number, and date when bought. This list should be regularly brought up to date so that replacement materials can be bought in good time. It is also necessary for insurance purposes, particularly when your materials are valuable e.g. silver and gold. A list of capital items including stock-in-hand and work-in-progress are counted as liquid assets of the business when drawing up the Accounts.

FILING

There are many filing systems, all of them fairly boring to keep going, but nevertheless time, space and chaos saving. Basically you need a filing cabinet, files, an 'In tray', an 'Out tray', and a waste paper bin.

Incoming mail should be placed in the 'In tray' if requiring attention, or filed in its appropriate file if not requiring a reply. Outgoing mail should always be typed on a letter headed sheet with a carbon copy. If the letter is part of an ongoing correspondence to which you are anxiously awaiting a reply, then the copy should be placed in a 'Pending' file. The 'In tray' and 'Pending' file should be regularly inspected to remind yourself of what has to be done, or who has not yet answered you.

TIME SHEET

For sensible pricing of your product or services, it is essential that, to begin with at least, you time yourself at work. Like the shock that often follows adding up the petty-cash and sundry items of expenditure, you will probably be amazed at the total of those few minutes here and there, particularly when a job is done in stages or batches. Gradually you will learn the time it takes you to make a hand-bag for example, but do not leave it to guess-work – you will almost undoubtedly underestimate.

VALUE ADDED TAX

You are not obliged to register as a VAT trader until your annual turnover has reached £10,000. Until you reach this point you will have to pay the extra 15% Tax on all materials subject to VAT, and will not be able to reclaim any of it unless you become a voluntary VAT trader. However, once your turnover has reached the current level appropriate, you will be entitled to charge VAT to your own customers, except on exported goods.

When making a return to Customs and Excise, the total VAT paid by you is set off against the total received by you from your customers. The difference is the amount paid by you to the Customs and Excise in the case of excess income, or to you by the Customs and Excise in the case of excess expenditure.

VAT is not simple, and it is advisable to seek the advice either of your accountant or your local Customs and Excise Office who have the responsibility of visiting registered persons in their own home area. HM Customs and Excise issue various guides on VAT including a general guide (No 700).

When All Else Fails

If reading a chapter like this makes you feel like lying down in a darkened room with a couple of aspirin, knowing in your heart that you just couldn't do it, there is still an answer. Find a Partner who can.

Golford Furnishings

Stewart and Dave run a business based on traditional methods of furniture-making and upholstery. Dave apprenticed as a boy in Hampstead, North London, as a furniture upholsterer, and then worked for various stores to build up his experience. The thought of all the necessary paper-work discouraged him from starting his own business, but when, a few years ago, he met Stewart who was quite able to cope with book-work, orders, customers etc, they decided that their personalities and skills were complementary, making an ideal partnership. It was in fact the meshing of the two characters that gave the initial impetous to the business rather than any practical advantages or considerations. Had they thought too much about the problems and realities of the situation, they said, they would probably never have taken the risk, especially as they had only £25 each with which to start. Now, however, they cannot imagine working in any other way. They rented a two room workshop in Deddington, Oxford, and began to carry out the three-weeks-worth of orders which they had on their books, ploughing every bit of money back into the business. Having so little money made them appreciate every thing they spent. Now 2½ years later they have built up to a comfortable living, and feel quite confident that they will achieve this goal. The pleasure derived from this business is primarily that of knowing that they are one of the few businesses which use traditional methods of making and refurbishing furniture, using springs, horse-hair, webbing and padding, which is tacked and hand-stitched, resulting in a piece of furniture that is not only elegant and beautiful, but will outlast by years most of todays mass-produced goods. To drive the point home, a bare plastic form of a modern arm-chair is balanced derisively on top of a pile of their materials like an effigy.

Dave also takes an evening class once a week in traditional upholstery for do-it-yourselfers who wish to rennovate their own furniture. This, Dave has found to be a good way to supplement his income, as have many others who have a skill which they are able to share. You do not have to be a qualified teacher to take an evening class, and many people who at one time thought that they were too shy, or incompetent to teach, have found that teaching actually gives you confidence and enjoyment.

Limited by Guarantee of What?

Chapter Four

Structures

CHAPTER FOUR: Structures

Limited by Guarantee of What?

There are several ways in which a person, or group of people can legally structure their working lives. For many of us the real meaning, implications and differences between the names we hear everyday to describe working relationships, e.g. Business and Company are vague and confusing, yet we are supposed to understand these without ever having had the terms explained to us. A basic understanding of the variety of structures available can help greatly when choosing how you wish to work.

Self-employed

If you intend to work on your own account, and are in a position to finance your project, and are willing to be personally liable for any debts you may incur, then the simplest structure for you is to become self-employed. This means that you virtually cut yourself off from the State except for the payment of Class 2 National Insurance Contributions (see Chapter 6 statutory regulations) bought at a special rate for the self-employed, from Post Office or debited directly from your Bank Account.

Business

If you intend to use a Trade name for your project other than your own 'true surname', then the law requires that, in addition to being self-employed, you register the name of the Business 'J Higginbotham', maker of Toys, would not require to be registered, but 'Higgy Toys' would. To register a business you write to the Registrar of Companies, Business Names and Limited Partnerships, Companies House, 55 City Road, London EC1. He will want to know the nature of the business, the name or names of the proprietor(s) and the proposed name of the business. This costs very little, and could save you a fine of several pounds a day if you fail to do it within fourteen days of formally opening your Office or Workshop. The Registrar will send you a certificate which you are obliged to frame and hang up in your 'registered office'. Again, failure to do this could result in a £20.00 fine. In addition, your letter-heading and any other printed material you distribute must show your 'true name', and that of any partners, as well as your registered business name.

Partnership

Legally speaking, the difference between two self-employed people working together, and a partnership, is what you decide it shall be. For example, if one

evening you were to sit over a pint or two with your best friend, and the conversation should go:
'Say, me 'ole mate, how about coming to work with me'. 'Right me 'ole chum, that's a great idea, I will'. 'Here's to us then, partners!' from that moment on, you could in fact be partners. A partnership would have been set up by a mutual verbal agreement, and that is all that is needed. However, these kind of agreements have a nasty habit of making things very confused, drawn out and ugly when best friends learn that their favourite drinking partner is a pain to work with, or some other disillusionment sets in, and you decide to part ways.

It is better that you look at each other right at the beginning as potential enemies and draw up a proper Partnership Agreement to be referred to in times of disagreement or dissolution. All that is required is written evidence that the Partnership exists, with details of the rights, duties and remuneration of the partners, and how the business shall be organised and managed. This can be written on any piece of paper by one or both of the partners, and the terms stated can be decided by the partners themselves, although it may be wise to have this professionally prepared by a solicitor or accountant. Both partners must sign the deed, and each partner should have a properly signed copy. In general the following provisions should be made:
(a) Name of the firm
(b) Nature of business
(c) How capital is to be provided
(d) How profits and losses are to be shared
(e) How drawings of money are to be regulated
(f) How accounts are to be kept
(g) The powers and duties of the individual partner
(h) What happens on dissolution, and under what conditions dissolution shall take place
(i) An arbitration clause so that in the event of a dispute independent persons can be appointed to settle it.

The deed is equally binding whether written by the partners or by a solicitor. If the name of the firm is not to consist of the 'true names' of the partners then the Registrar of Companies and Limited Partnerships must be informed.

Limited Company

The advantage of a Limited Company is that it is the legal creation of a 'third person' who is liable for all your debts. It is 'limited' because the liability it has for debts is limited by the amount of money you decide to put into it. Therefore, in the dreaded event of bankruptcy, you cannot be ordered to sell your private possessions to pay your creditors. It is a safer structure. It is also more complicated than the previous three.

A Company must have:
(1) At least two shareholders

(2) At least one director (who can be a shareholder)

(3) A secretary (who could be your accountant or solicitor).

To form a Company, you can ask a Solicitor, or use a Company registration agent. They are mainly found in Central London, and will do all the legal work for a smaller charge than a Solicitor, although both are quite expensive (£50.00 or more).

You must submit:

(a) A Memorandum which sets out the main objects of the Company. The nominal capital is divided into shares. There must be two shareholders, even if one holds only one share.

(b) Articles of Association, setting out the rules of the internal affairs of the Company.

Upon registration you will receive:

(a) A certificate of Incorporation – your licence. This must be displayed in your Registered Office

(b) A Company seal

(c) A Minute book

(d) Share transfer forms to issue to the Shareholders.

Companies have distinct advantages when it comes to raising money, as it is easier to find people willing to buy shares than willing to become partners and to incur all the liabilities which a partner incurs.

A Co-operative

The co-operative movement was originally a direct rebellion by the workers against both the control of their work and the profit from it being in the hands of people whose qualification to do this were solely that they owned the shares. In an ordinary Company, the main policy decisions as to the management of the Company are made at meetings of the shareholders. Shareholders voting power is in direct proportion to the amount of shares owned. Thus it is legally possible for a rich investor who has bought 51% of the shares in a Company to outvote all the rest of shareholders on any matter, including dissolution, although he may be a stranger living miles away and having no concern or knowledge of the well-being of his 'employees'. He will also be the main beneficiary of a rise in the value of his shares if the Company becomes successful even though the workers, not he, have been responsible for this success.

A workers co-operative is different in structure from such a Company in that whilst still having shares, and limited liability, the voting control is on a one-man-one-vote principle, regardless of the number of shares owned. Another co-operative principle is that the return on capital is limited, and by law a co-op cannot pay a dividend on its shares at more than a certain rate above the Bank of England minimum lending rate. Consequently, if the employed members of a co-operative work hard to make it successful, they must benefit themselves from the prosperity they have earned, rather than the shareholders reaping unlimited rewards.

A co-operative is governed by rules as opposed to the memorandum and Articles of Association of an Incorporated Company, and is registered under the industrial and Provident Societies Act 1965-75, and not the Companies Acts, 1948-67. A co-operative pays Corporation Tax at a reduced rate compared to a company.

'Little Women'

'Little Women' is a small workers' co-operative initiated by seven mothers or young children who wanted to be involved in some kind of paid employment, but who also did not want to miss out on the early years of their childrens' development.

They decided to open a shop of the old-fashioned 'Corner Shop' type, an alternative to the supermarket, in which two eggs, or a listening ear could be found again.

It took two years to raise the money they needed to start. After being turned down by several Banks, this eventually came from a bank loan from Charitable Trusts and from individual donations from supporters, amounting to a total of eight thousand pounds. With this capital they were able to lease a three storey shop. On the first floor they had a nursery and kitchen, and on the second floor they had flats which they let, the rent from which helped to pay back the bank loan.

Being a co-operative, they manage their business in weekly committee meetings at which time the weekly rota is worked out. As they sell dried whole-foods as well as other groceries, they also have to arrange to pick up their stocks from the wholesalers.

After the first six months, they were all receiving a wage and were paying off their bank loan. Two girls had left and two had joined. They advised similar groups to get to know each other well, particularly at the beginning, when the willingness to work hard is so important. From their experience they realise that housewives could open almost anything like this depending on the interests and skills owned by the members of the group — hairdressers, restaurants and so on. The key to success will be providing a service in an area in which it is needed.

New Forms of Work

The structure of co-operation which calls for the bringing together of several like-minded people can give 'Creating your own work' a further dimension. It often happens that a group of people will find the courage to do things too daunting for an individual, such as forming entirely new forms of work which express perhaps beliefs which are not expressed in any conventional work situation. Examples of this kind of innovation amongst co-operatives includes an Alternative Computer Bureau in which two self-taught computer operators bought two vintage computers, the services of which they made available to 'ordinary' people including school and college students, and a musical co-operative producing records that popularise progressive ideas, and low-cost, short-run issues of records made by community groups to publicise musically their particular activity.

Publications

'In the making' is a directory of co-operative projects that are already functioning, or in the process of being set-up. Apart from bristling with stimulating ideas and useful information, this publication is a resourse in which you can ask for support for your own project, particularly if you need more people to join you. It is available from 'Acorn' 84 Church Street, Wolverton, Milton Keynes, Berks.

The members of Uhuru, a co-operative wholefood shop have written about their experiences in 'Uhuru, a Working Alternative', which includes describing the psychological barriers that at first make it difficult to assign oneself tasks which society has hitherto assigned only to 'experts', and the sense of confidence which comes from overcoming the barriers. It costs 60p and is available from Uhuru, 53 Cowley Road, Oxford.

Common Ownership

Scott-Bader set a precedent when, on retiring he gave his firm, a flourishing concern, to his employees in gratitude for the effort they had made, and loyalty they had shown during years of set-backs and difficulties. It became the Scott-Bader Commonwealth, and marked a step further even than a workers co-operative, as all the shares were owned by the people working in it. The condition on which he handed over the firm was that they applied strict percentages of their profits, firstly to a general reserve for the continuation and development of the firm, secondly to a bonus for members, and thirdly to a social or charitable cause.

These new principles greatly appealed to many people who believed that work should not be based on purely capitalistic values, but on the benefit derived by the common-good. Some of these copied the example made by Scott-Bader, and as the number of such enterprises grew, the Industrial Common Ownership Movement, (ICOM) developed to spread the principles of Common Ownership and to support new ventures.

On November 2nd 1976, the Industrial Common Ownership Bill became an Act and the law of the Land, releasing Government Funds to assist the growth of the movement.

ICOM have subsequently published a 'launching kit' called 'How to form an Industrial Co-operative' which consists of a folder containing copies of Model Rules, drawn up to incorporate co-operative and common-ownership principles, amended in July 1977 to comply with the Industrial Common Ownership Act. The Folder contains also all the forms required for registration and a comprehensive booklet – 'Industrial Co-operatives, a guide to the ICOM Model Rules'. Under these rules, if you wanted to start a co-operative enterprise, you would first have to find at least six friends to join you. The capital would be donated or loaned to the enterprise, but would not be owned by any of the members, except for one share each, costing £1.00, non-transferable and non-redeemable. Members can of course lend their money. Distribution of profits would be along the lines of Scott-Baders initiative, and the enterprise could only be dissolved by the assent of at least $\frac{3}{4}$ of the members. If any assets remain on the dissolution of the co-operative, after the payment of all liabilities, they must be transferred to other co-operatives or charities. Registration under the Act costs (1977) £27.00 and can be completed in about a month. The model rules are short and simple and are designed to give members as much freedom as possible to decide for themselves the conditions they wish to impose upon themselves. The 'launching kit' is available free to new Associate members of ICOM, or to anyone for the cost of £5.00 from ICOM, Beechwood Hall, Minute Lane, Leeds 8. Certificates of registration under the Act are available from the Registrar of Friendly Societies, 17 North Audley Street, London W1Y 2AP.

A Charity

We are not totally powerless to put right some of the wrong we see around us. If the work you wish to create is of such a nature that its prime object is to help others rather than yourselves, then it is possible to form yourselves into a charity. A charity is basically a non-profit making organisation, which means that after overheads and after the payment of salaries to staff, all remaining monies must go to help further the objects and aims of the charity. The main advantage of becoming a registered charity is that it makes accessible part of the amazing £2 million dispensed each year by grant-giving Trusts. The meaning of the word 'Charity' is gradually changing from the concept of alms-giving to the 'poor and needy' by the 'rich and bountiful', to mean the organisation of resources for purposes other than financial gain, or political power, which are not provided by the State. John may have the money to help organise a Toy Library, but not the time, whereas Mabel has the time but not the money. If the two manage to communicate and to pool their resources, the Toy Library materialises.

A charity has several differences in structure from either a company or a co-operative. Firstly, it does not have limited liability, and the Trustees are legally the 'Guarantors' of all loans, and are liable for all debts incurred by the Charity.

Secondly, the business is in the hands of the members who pay subscriptions to the charity. Each year at the Annual General Meeting, they elect from the members a Committee of Management to run the affairs of the organisation, according to the constitution and rules accepted by the Charity Commission as legally charitable.

Thirdly, as a general rule, it is not acceptable for members of staff to vote at committee meetings. This is to make sure that the members of the committee do not have a 'vested interest' in any decision made. It is also not acceptable for members to personally benefit from any income, over and above that due to them for salaries and all reasonable expenses, whether the income be from grants or trading.

Dual Structures

However, this apparent rigidity, which seems to frustrate any attempts disadvantaged people may make towards self-help, can be adapted for many purposes by the addition of, or amalgamation with, a second structure. A charity can become a 'Limited Company with Charitable status having no share capital', meaning that it can enjoy the protection of limited liability, and alleviating the Trustees of the responsibility for debts.

A workers co-operative can also become a charity, able to raise capital from charitable sources, if the members belong to an underprivileged group. Rowen-Onllwyn in Wales is an engineering co-operative set up by a group of unemployed disabled miners. They have a two-tier structure consisting of a Trading Company, and a Charitable 'Holding' Company. This is to resolve a dilemma caused by the fact that a co-operative is not a co-operative unless democratically controlled by its working members, whilst a charity cannot be controlled by its employees. The two-tier structure means that the workers have decided to place the financial affairs of their Trading Company in the hands of a charitable 'Holding' Company, which happens to consist of the same people.

A third important dual structure is that of a charity having a trading subsidiary. This means that a Trading Company covenants its profits to a linked charity so that the charity can reclaim the income tax paid on the profits and use the whole sum to further its aims. This way you are in fact choosing how the tax you pay on your own earnings are spent. The following example will illustrate this.

JEAN DAVIS. THE BURNBAKE TRUST
Jean Davis began her project a few years ago when she was a voluntary prison visitor. Seeing that many of the prisoners were bored, she began a jewellery-making scheme to give them an interest that would both use their creativity, and earn a little extra money for Christmas. Everyone said she was mad, it wouldn't last more than two weeks and so on, but by Christmas the project had been running for eight months and had made £500 profit. Jean had sold the jewellery in her spare time by taking it round to craft shops. The whole venture

suddenly took a swing from being a pastime to being a serious affair when a change in family circumstances meant she had to support herself and her children. Turning to her 'mad' project as a means of survival, she established with housewives and some discharged prisoners, Jean Davis Crafts Limited, making and selling bead jewellery. As her experience grew, so did the profitability of the company. Soon she was able to employ an agent to sell the jewellery on a commission basis.

Jean believes that crime is one of the most misunderstood phenomena of our Society, and to further her belief she set up the Burnbake Trust in 1975 to help prisoners resume their place in society by providing them with the moral support, advice and training in handi-crafts. In return they give her friendship. The Burnbake Trust is a charity funded by Covenanting the profits of Jean Davis Crafts Ltd, as well as public grants and donations. With the extra income she has been able to buy 'Burnbake', two houses made into one, where she lives with her family and several ex-offenders, as well as running the jewellery work-shop.

Many readers of this book will have seen in craft shops their unique 'horse-shoe' nail jewellery, made mostly by male ex-offenders. The jewellery is a revival of an old gypsy craft based on the legend that the pendants, made of bent horse-shoe nails soldered or wired together, are tokens of fertility given to a man by his wife when they marry. If the man is unfaithful, the nails unbend and pierce his heart. The Trust are now developing a new offset-litho printing project, making prints from the art work of prisoners, which are then framed and sold. The artists receive a royalty on each print sold, as well as the security of knowing that they have a visible trade which can be continued when they are released. The project is funded by the Manpower Services Commission, the equipment bought by the Home Office and is led by a live-wire fresh from Art College girl called Carol. Jean well deserves to feel, as she does, a great sense of achievement. She now has twelve agents selling approximately £100's worth of jewellery a week. She says that now she is glad of the difficult situation in which she had been left, as it made her do things for herself. 'All this' she said, 'from beads!'

Setting Up a Charity

To set up a charity, you must first find a group of people who are also interested, willing to act as the committee. You must have a Chairman, Secretary, and Treasurer who will be the Officers' of the Committee. You must work out between you, your aims, who are to be the beneficiaries of your charity, and the Rules of the Association. To help you with this, it is useful to obtain a copy of Model Rules. The National Council of Social Services, 26 Bedford Square, London WC1, will give any group wishing to form themselves into a charity, advice and guidance on these matters. A solicitor will also draw up for you a 'Constitution and Rules according to Charity Law', but this can be expensive. If however, you wish operate locally, then you need only apply for registration as a local charity with your Local Authorities. If however, you wish to operate in a wider area, or make appeals for funds outside your locality, then you must register as a National Charity with the Charity Commission, 17 Ryder Street, London. They will want to see your Constitution and Rules, and copies of your latest audited accounts if you have any. You will then have to wait for anything up to a year before they issue you with a registration number. The Charity Commission will want to see your audited accounts at the end of the financial year, and have the right to strike you off the list if they have, by way of complaints and investigation, deemed your activities to be no longer legally charitable.

Working Communities

If you like the company of other people, but only up to a point, then a place in a working community may be for you. Working communities are a recent development which have evolved to bridge the gap between working as an isolated individual or group, and the essentially more intense and demanding structure of the co-operative or charity. They are basically a collection of small independent firms, and self-employed people who have joined together to share a building and usually some joint facilities. Each firm or person retains their independence and identity, and so does not become subject to the risks involved in more interdependent, closely knit groups. The main aim is for the collection of small independent firms to enjoy, by their joint purchasing power, a scale of premises and facilities normally only enjoyed by larger firms. In addition to this main advantage, are several others: the provision of exactly the working space you need, at an economic rent, with security of tenure; the ability to expand or contract as circumstances demand, without having to change address; the creation of better working conditions; the ability to share various joint services, equipment and machinery; the company, stimulation and support of other people. An important point about this kind of organisation is that usually the originators make use of some of the large number of empty buildings in our inner-city areas which have been left to rot. Some workshops have been originated by a Building Preservation Trust which can obtain charitable status.

Clerkenwell Workshops

The Business and Industry award was given in 1976 to the Clerkenwell Workshops, in recognition of social responsibility and environmental quality. They were founded in January, 1976 and consisted of 6000 square metres of workshop space. It was bought by a small developing Company and structured to be non-profit making. Funding came from Charitable Grants and loans, an overdraft and personal capital. After carrying out repairs, fire-proofing, electrical re-fitting, supply of main services, and partitioning, the building has been let to 85 individual firms providing employment for approximately 160 men and 120 women. These units vary from a one man jewellery-making business, to an eight-man spectacle-frame manufacturing firm. Each tenant is issued with a license which entitles him to a defined square footage of space, but not in a specified place. There is an agreement that no changes of occupation of workshop spaces take place without the general consent of the majority of the fellow tenants. All tenants share building services − heating, electricity, gas, sprinklers, management services (informal help from the Crafts Director and reception services), and communal facilities − canteen, extra storage, large teaching workshop, meeting/rehearsal/exhibition spaces to hire. Payment for all these services, apart from electricity and gas, are included in the surprisingly low rent. Everyone pays a set amount of rent per square foot occupied. Almost all the tenants have some kind of link with others in the building. Some 'production lines' link five or six separate trades.

401 ½ Workshop

Michael Haynes was responsible for the setting up of the 401 ½ Workshop in Wandsworth, London, and the related Fosseway House Workshop in Gloucestershire.

He is primarily interested in helping young artist/craftsman to begin their career, the aim of his workshops being to promote the very highest level of work. The 401 ½ workshop (its street number!) was founded in April 1970 and consists of 1000 square metres of space let to 50 designer/craftsmen who were all selected and invited to join the group. They take the space they need, but all pay the same rent of £5.00 (1977) a week. This rent includes all services and use of common facilities such as kilns, dark-room and use of light industrial machinery. Fosseway House workshops are run on the same basis, but also provide living accommodation in a late Victorian Cotswold Manor House. They began in late 1975 when eight people moved in and began to convert the house, a process which has gone on ever since. At the present time there are thirteen residents, ranging from a ceramic musical instrument maker, to The Blue Nose Press-fine Art photo-silkscreen printers. They find that they give each other the mental and physical support to carry them through the early days of hard grind and shaky confidence which so often defeat the lone craftsman.

Barley Mow Workspace

The Barley Mow Workspace Limited, using the same principles, have made their 3,300 square metres available to 100 member firms. These firms pay a little more than the previous examples in return for more sophisticated communal facilities.

47

Barley Mow offer not only workshop space, but also space for design/studio/office accommodation, and the service charge includes telephone installation and rental, leasing of communally used furniture, telex rental, management staff salaries including switchboard operator and receptionist, and use of conference ooms. A canteen is also provided initially through central funding, but eventually by a service company. In the same way printing, xeroxing and secretarial services are made available. Member firms which use these facilities include consultant engineers, a charitable Trust, illustrators and graphic designers, architects, a translation agency, and a tour operator. Workshop space is used by craftsmen, fashion designers and a teacher of the Alexander Technique.

THE FEDERATION OF WORKING COMMUNITIES is a loose association of people involved in, or interested in, working communities. It was formed to share the experiences they have gained, and to support, encourage, and promote the concept. Further details about the Federation can be obtained from the acting honorary Secretary, 5 Dryden Street, Covent Garden, London, WC0 9NW.

But Will Anybody Buy It?

chapter Five Marketing

CHAPTER FIVE: Marketing

But Will Anybody Buy It?

If an article is well designed and well made, then it should not be difficult to sell. Likewise, if you propose to offer people a service which you do well, and at a competitive rate, then you should not be lacking for custom.

However, for people who are inexperienced in the world of advertising and selling, there are two problems which can seem baffling.

Firstly, how to properly cost your product or service, and secondly how to find your market.

Costing

When costing your product or service, there are three main considerations to be made.

To begin, you need to work out what the article has cost you to make. In the chapter on additional skills, the importance of keeping detailed records of all raw materials used, was mentioned. The total cost of raw materials should be divided by the number of articles your materials made. Added to this should be a proportion of your overheads, and any other items of expense, such as petrol or advertising, which must be paid for from the profits of your work.

Having arrived at this basic cost, decide on the profit margin you wish to make. This will depend to a large degree on the time it takes you to complete the task. For example, imagine you can make 10 units for £100, or £10 each, and it takes you two hours to make one unit. You may decide that you could make 4 units a day, and that you could be content earning £40 per week, or £8 per day. You need therefore to make £2 profit on each unit, so your final selling price is fixed at £10 + £2 = £12 each.

If, however, you could make one unit in 10 minutes, then you could make 48 in one day, and your profit margin need only be 1/48th of £8 = approx 18p.

The third consideration to make is to determine what is already on the market of a similar type and quality to the one you propose, and what prices they are already commanding. If, for example your ambition is to make yak-wool rugs, for which you must charge a minimum of £30 each, and in your local craft-shop there are yak-wool rugs imported from Tibet where there are swarms of Yaks, being sold for £6.50, then you are obviously going to have difficulty selling yours. If, however, there are no yak-wool rugs imported from Tibet, if they are not even made in Tibet, and most hand-woven rugs you can find for sale are selling for £35 each, or more, then you know you can afford to widen your profit margin a little, and start planning that holiday you thought you were not going to be able to afford.

When balancing these two factors – your required profit margin, and the apparent potential selling price – you must remember to decide to whom, or through whom you are going to sell – a wholesaler, retailer, exhibitions, an agent, or directly to the customer through advertising, stalls, private word-of-mouth orders, or mail-order. Each method requires different considerations, and should be costed and added to your overheads when working out your prices.

A wholesaler is really only interested in bulk buying. He will sell his stock to retailers at a profit. The retailers will sell to the public at a profit, therefore there will be a vast difference between the price he pays you, and the price of the article which is finally charged to the customer. The advantage is that if you are a small manufacturing enterprise that has stumbled on a way to stamp out thousands of one article, a wholesaler will take off your hands the difficult and time-consuming task of distribution. If you sell direct to a retailer, then you are the producer/wholesaler.

A retailer will add anything from 60%-100% on the price of your goods, and this must be taken into account when comparing your hoped-for price to those of similar goods on sale in shops.

Exhibitions and galleries also charge a commission on work sold. Often they also have a basic standing charge. However, many private orders can come from exhibitions for which, of course, you can receive the full amount you ask. Exhibitions are invaluable publicity. An agent will charge a percentage of all the work of yours he sells, but the good news is that he has to sell it before he gets paid. Advertising costs varying amounts of money. Stalls require the payment of rent, and mail-order requires advertising, postage and packing. The time taken to sell the goods must also be taken into account. If you spend one day a month travelling in your car from shop to shop, then the loss of earnings, plus petrol and any other expenses, should be added to your overheads.

Services, as opposed to manufacturing ventures, are usually costed by the hour. The higher your qualifications, the more you can expect to charge. The rule here is to find out what other people are charging. If, for example, you are starting a Home Typing Service, then ring up your local typing agency and find out their current charges. As they will most likely have higher overheads than you to contend with, you will probably be able to charge a slightly lower fee, thus attracting custom on your way. Remember not to charge too low a fee as this will only result in people thinking you must be rubbish. Finally, if you believe your service or product is unique and so not comparable with anything else, then you must charge what you feel you need to live on, and hope for the best.

Selling

There are no hard and fast rules about selling your services or products. All the following methods have been successfully employed by the different people who have contributed to this book, and often it was a combination of two or more methods which eventually won the day.

Advertising

To bring yourself to the attention of your market you can place a one-off or regular advertisement in your local newspaper, national newspaper, or in an appropriate trade journal. A list of trade journals is published by Business Publications Limited, called the 'Advertiser's Annual', and should be in your local reference Library. Make your advertisements as original as possible if you really want to attract attention to your business.

Another form of advertising is to have a 'New Address' or Business Card printed which you can send to absolutely everyone who may be a potential customer.

Make sure your Business name is in the Yellow Pages of the Telephone Directory. Even accountants and solicitors, who are not usually allowed to advertise, may do this.

Also, do not overlook local custom which can be obtained by placing an advertisement on a postcard in a shop window.

Retailers

Many people interviewed had originally sold their work by sorting out suitable shops, ringing up the proprietor or store buyer, and asking for an appointment at which they could show samples of their work. Unfortunately, unless you are an established 'best seller', most shops will only take work on a sale or return basis. This means you may have to wait a long time for a return on your work, which will not give you the immediate cash you may need to buy your next lot of materials. If however, you find a shop which agrees to buy your work outright, you have found a treasure.

To move from hawking your wares through other people's shops, to opening a shop of your own, is not as difficult a step as you may imagine.

MICHAEL & HEATHER ACKLAND, JEWELLERS
Michael was a biologist at Oxford University when he started to be interested in making jewellery. He began to read books on silver-smithing and practised with simple tools at home. After a while he sold a few pieces to friends, and with the money bought himself more tools and materials. He took his examples to shops, and gradually began to fill his evenings and weekends by fulfilling private orders as well as continuing to supply his few retail outlets.

After three years of doing this, he found he was earning more in his spare time than at his job, at which point he decided to leave the university in order to become a full time jeweller.

He also taught his wife to make jewellery, and together they moved into a little shop with workspace in the back, living in the flat above. They originally stocked that shop with a large variety of crafts, as well as their own products, but gradually diminished the range to pottery and jewellery only, without suffering any financial loss. The less expensive crafts were, they felt, detracting from the jewellery by making false comparisons, whilst the pottery is of an equal standard and price range, making a complementary display.

Neither Michael nor Heather had had any experience of running a shop but they now consider it an easy task providing they have some taste and style when choosing stock, and that they as shop-keepers are nice to their customers. They also pointed out that unless you are situated in the middle of a teeming shopping metropolis, it takes a long time for people to realise you are there. They believe it will take them about five years to become really established in the area.

Being craftsmen themselves, they are aware of the difficulties caused to other craftsmen by the practice of selling on a sale-or-return basis, and they always buy their stock outright and then re-sell it. Much of their bread-and-butter money comes from making large quantities of simple ear-studs and rings which they still sell to many other shops apart from their own. These, however, they find boring to make and are pleased, after having built up a stock, to be free to work on their own individual and more creative designs. All their jewellery is modestly priced to within the price-range of the general public, and is not aimed at an exclusive market.

They have used agents to sell their work in the past, but now do it all themselves. Michael feels that this way he has more control of what, and how much, work he is committed to do. If, for example, he wishes to design pendants for the next two weeks, then he can run down his orders for other things. In addition to this, he believes that the contact between himself – the craftsman – and the buyer, has a psychological effect, which results in his being paid more quickly. The travelling involved, of course, adds extra interest and variety to his life, and while he restricts his 'hunting ground' to the South of England, the cost of the petrol involved is less than would be the agents' fees. However, the advantage of having an agent in a more remote part of the country is something they are considering for the future.

Michael is someone who would rather make his own mistakes than suffer through those of someone else. Like many others, he enjoys not having anyone in authority over him, in spite of the fact that this means the entire responsibility for success or failure rests on the shoulders of his wife and himself.

Galleries, Stalls, Exhibitions, Trade Fairs

Many people have begun their trading life on a rickety stall at a Fete, Craft Fair, Trade Fair, or in a market place. The first three require you to keep your eyes peeled and your ears flapping to discover any forthcoming events in your area, the organiser of which you can then immediately ring up and ask for space.

Stalls in market places are not so easy to come by, particularly in the more popular sites. Enquiries about sites should be made through your local Council. The Town Hall will put you in touch with the right department. They will also send you an application form for a Street Traders Licence which they may, or may not grant you. People who are of a strong enough constitution to withstand the rising at dawn, the loading and unloading of the stall, the rain and the winds, can make a good living either buying and selling other people's goods, and/or their own. Indoor markets are privately owned and the manager or owner should be approached with enquiries. The 'Markets Year Book' published by World's Fair Ltd, Union Street, Oldham, can be found in most reference libraries, and is a useful source of information about rules and regulations with lists of markets and wholesalers. For the craftsmen among you, galleries are often the best way of bringing your work out of the workshop and into the hands of the public. They attract a clientele who are interested, and prepared to pay for quality goods. The manager of a good gallery can often be the best agent for your work. However, like many shops, they put a high mark-up, up to 100%, on your exhibits, and sell on a sale-or-return basis. For a list of galleries open to craftsmen see 'Museums and Galleries in Great Britain & Ireland', ABC Travel Guides Limited, Oldhill, Dunstable, Bedfor; or the *Arts Review Yearbook and Directory*' obtainable from Richard Gainsborough Periodicals Ltd, 8 Wyndham Place, London W1. 'Crafts', a bi-monthly magazine published by the Crafts Advisory Committee, 12 Waterloo Place, London SW1, has a calendar of craft exhibitions throughout the Country.

Turrets Gallery, 37 Friern Barnet Road, London N11, is Barnet Borough Arts Council's attempt to make inexpensive gallery space available to artists and craftsmen who man their own exhibitions for a mere 15% commission payable to the Council on work sold.

Exhibitions of craft work are held by local and national craft associations and guilds. Naturally, to belong to one of these associations you must have achieved an acceptable standard. Most of them are linked to the Crafts Advisory Council who will put you in touch with your nearest or most relevant group.

As the selection committees of these organisations require high standards of their members, and even once having accepted you as a member, will accept or reject individual items of your work for exhibitions, the very achievement of becoming an exhibiting member can be a weighty recommendation of your work to the public. A declaration of membership should be stated on all your publicity and advertisements. The exhibitions tend to attract sympathetic clientele, and some invite foreign buyers. Success at these events can often be the launching pad for people, even when other methods have failed.

TIM AND SUE CURRANT
Tim and Sue live in Devon and both had undertaken Art Courses at Dartington

College (see Chapter Two) where Tim continued to work as a technical assistant for three years.

During this period Sue began to make patchwork quilts, silk-screen printing the patches herself. She soon found that to make the time available to develop this craft, as well as other ideas that were fermenting, she would have to leave her own job. She applied to the Crafts Advisory Committee for a grant under their 'New Craftsmen' scheme. For this she was asked to submit slides of her work, and a written paper on what she hoped to do with the grant if she were to get it. She was also expected to already have a definite place from which to work. Having decided from these entries that she was interesting enough, the CAC invited her up to London for an interview, as a result of which she was awarded a maintenance grant for one year. The CAC are also empowered to award up to half the cost of any equipment needed.

With this backing Sue was able to make patchwork cushions and smocks, selling a few samples to shops. She found however, that she could not support herself by doing this.

The urge to make something was still strong in both Sue and Tim. They felt that if perhaps they worked together, they might be more successful, so Tim left his job at Dartington, and they began to make and sell highly detailed dolls' houses. Unfortunately, they were so detailed that the time involved was too great to make the venture economical, and they began to worry about what to do next.

As it happened, while they were doing all this, they had made some presents of wooden boxes with hand-sewn patchwork lids. Being members of the Devonshire Guild of Craftsmen, they had been invited to exhibit their dolls houses, to which they thought they might add a few of the boxes for the sake of variety. To their surprise, the boxes sold very well. Realising that they might have found the product that would 'take off', they obtained some more sophisticated woodworking equipment to speed up their production and, encouraged by their success at the exhibition, they took the boxes on a selling trip to shops.

From this trip they obtained just enough orders to keep them going. Their second selling trip took them all over the South of England and, resulting from that, steady orders began to roll in. They employ one outworker to help with the sewing of the patchwork, and believe that very soon they will be ready to expand further.

Sue and Tim have a young baby daughter who needs constant attention during the day, consequently most of Sue's work has to be done in the evening. The determination to succeed despite the disappointments and sacrifices they have had to make comes partly from a fairly universal desire to disprove the forebodings of their sceptical friends and relatives, and to demonstrate a serious attempt to live the life they choose. They enjoy the challenge and cannot imagine earning their livings in any way other than by making and selling craftwork.

What Can I Do Myself?

There is still a great need for local initiatives in terms of selling, publicising and exhibiting the work of tiny businesses and lone craftsmen, particularly when they are newcomers to the fields of industry and commerce, have no experience, and little confidence. People often need to test out the saleability of their products before deciding whether to make it a full-time commitment. There is a great deal you can do to help yourself, and others over this problem.

ANNE HOFFMAN

Anne Hoffman is a designer and maker of soft toys, a business which has enabled her to support herself from home despite being a sufferer from chronic asthma. Realising that the lack of confidence new craftsmen often feel is due to not knowing whether other people will like their product, Anne started to organise craft fairs where she lives in Newbury.

All the people who participate, create hand-made goods of a high standard. They not only exhibit their work, but also talk to the public about their techniques and give demonstrations; this all helps to boost their personal confidence, and to connect the craftsmen with their individual products in the minds of the potential local customers. The craft fairs are also something of a social event, enabling craftsmen to meet each other and their neighbours. This can make a tremendous difference to loners struggling along in their sheds or lofts, each feeling that he must be the only self-employed person in the world.

MUSTARD SEED

In Old Coulsdon in Surrey, an initiative has been taken by two women, Mailie and Ann, as a result of a church event. The event – an exhibition of local crafts – brought so much undiscovered talent to light, that the organisers felt they had to do something more permanent to encourage this talent.

They took a tiny room in the Church each Saturday, where they continued to exhibit and sell the work of about ten different people. Soon, more and more people heard of it, coming with samples of their work. Eventually the two women had to look for bigger premises in which to set it all out.

A local farmer finally offered them the use of a large empty barn, rent-free, asking only for the electricity to be paid. They gladly took the barn and moved all the crafts, paying only for insurance and for the occasional extra trestle-table.

They called themselves 'Mustard Seed' and advertised their whereabouts by means of a printed hand-out and articles in the local press. Many people are regular visitors to the barn, including both customers and craftsmen, now numbering over seventy, all of whom participate to some degree in the running of 'Mustard Seed'.

As their overheads are almost non-existent, the mark-up on goods is exceptionally low, only 20%. In addition to the crafts, farm produce is sold, and demonstrations of spinning and weaving are a regular attraction. As well as all this, 'Mustard Seed' is a rural-style haven from the noise and rush of the busy urban shopping centre which is only about $\frac{1}{4}$ of a mile away. To reach the barn you must leave the car at the end of the lane, walk past the horses and other farm animals, breathe lungs-full of heady farm air, before arriving at the bright, festooned building where often the church folk-singing group can be heard practising round a table, happy to have anyone join them. Mailie also takes spinning and weaving classes once a week in the barn. Her ambition, is to start 'Mustard Seed' everywhere.

CO-OPERATIVE MARKETS

For men and women who would like to earn some extra money from the produce of their gardens, kitchens or hands generally, the Women's Institute run Co-operative Markets in many towns and villages which are easily accessible to rural producers. They are registered under the Industrial and Provident Societies Act, and men and women who are not members of the WI can apply to become shareholders and sell their produce through the market, providing that their produce reaches the high standard required.

The markets are usually held one morning a week, selling home-made cakes, jams, breads, fresh vegetables, flowers, crafts and also providing a friendly meeting place.

Producers should, however, be prepared to help in the running of the markets.

A list of addresses and times of opening of those at present in operation can be obtained from the Market Adviser, The National Federation of Women's Institutes, 39 Eccleston Street, London SW1W 9NT.

Export

It is a big world, and many people who produce specialised goods often find they have to look farther afield than the British Coastline to find a suitable market.

In other countries of course, living standards and 'the value of the pound' vary significantly from ours, and this can mean that, in spite of the extra complications involved, exporting your goods results in receiving considerably more money for them.

Finding a market abroad can be done personally, acting as your own agent, or through a friend who lives overseas or who is willing to try his luck with your products whilst on holiday or travelling. Some exhibitions and Trade Fairs in this country attract foreign buyers who may order your wares, and embassies, or their trade delegations, can provide commercial contacts in their particular countries. There are also a number of buying houses which supply overseas customers. For crafts, a small company called 'Mantor Export Services', at 26 Hockerill Street, Bishops Stortford, Hertfordshire, specialises in 'Finding sales outlets throughout the World for the British Craft Industries'. They deal with the entire course of events from collection of the goods to recovering the payment from the customer.

'Export Made Easy', published by CoSIRA, 35 Camp Road, Wimbledon, SW19, is a guide which helps you to realise that although exporting goods can seem terribly complicated, like many things, once broken down into stages or a sequence of events, it is well within your capabilities.

Transportation

Post

If possible, it is easiest to send your goods by surface or air-mail in the same way as you would send a gift to a friend. The Post Office Guide, at 20p, is available from most Post Offices, and will give you all the information you need to know about rates, insurance, packing etc. For special inquiries ring the Post Office Information Service – 01.606 9876.

Rail

British Rail runs an international express parcel delivery service which covers most destinations in Europe. See the Parcel Sales Office at most main-line stations, or City Link Transport Services Limited, Kings Cross Freight Terminal, York Way, London N1.

Shipping

If your load is too large for posting, or putting on a train, then the more complicated procedure of shipping will have to be undertaken. For this you need to employ the services of a Shipping Agent whom you will find in the yellow pages of the Telephone Directory. To the price of your goods you will have to add the cost of packing, preparation of documents, transport to docks (or airport) dock dues or airport handling charges and the Shipping Agents Commission – around 5% of Ocean/Air Freight. You will not, however, have to charge VAT.

The most important new terms you will have to know are:

EX WORKS. The basic selling price of your commodity before any costs have been added.

F.O.B. (Free on Board) This is ex works price plus all costs up to placing the goods on board ship at the named port. e.g. FOB Southampton.

C. & F. (Cost & Freight) F.O.B. plus freight, e.g. C & F New York.

C.I.F. (Cost Insurance and Freight) FOB plus insurance & Freight. e.g. CIF Amsterdam.

When working out an estimated invoice for an overseas customer, you must work out your ex works price, and your FOB price. With this information plus the size and weight of the crates in which your goods are packed (unless they have undertaken to do this job also) your shipping agent will be able to give you the CIF prices, and you will be able to tell your customer what he will have to pay. The best way to do this is by a *pro-forma* invoice (specimen invoice) which should be clearly marked as such, so there is no confusion when you send the real invoice. At the foot of the *pro-forma* there should be a clause stating 'All increases in freight rates are for buyer's account'. Your shipping agent will send you a consignment note which you fill in, after which he will book your cargo on a space in a boat or cargo container, and he will either collect your goods, or tell you where and when to deliver them to the docks.

The agent will later send you a bill of lading (a receipt from the shipowner accepting your goods for delivery), insurance certificates and his bill. If you are trading on an open account, which means hoping to get paid on receipt of the goods, the Bill of Lading will be sent to your customer. Otherwise your customer will be paying 'Cash against Documents', which means that you send the lading bill, insurance certificates, invoice and sight draft (or bill of exchange) to your bank with instructions to forward them all to your customer's bank. On payment of the invoice by the customer, he will receive all the necessary documents he needs as an importer to claim his goods.

Self-delivery

If you are exporting to Europe, it may be easier, more lucrative, and a great deal more exciting, to deliver the goods yourself. If you intend to do this then you should read the 'Export Handbook' available from the British Overseas Trade Board, 1 Victoria St, London SW1, which has a very useful section 'Taking Goods Abroad in Your Own Vehicle', giving much basic information on the various cards, documents and permits you will need, and from where they may be obtained. If you are taking goods overseas only temporarily, for an exhibition for example, the procedure can be simplified. For details of this your local Customs and Excise Office should be approached.

Road-Haulage

For those of you who would rather pay extra to allow someone else to do all the work, The Road Haulage Association, 22 Upper Woburn Place, London WC1, have details of direct road services to Europe. A shipping agent can arrange for a a through transport service using one of these.

Packing

One's mind can often go blank when thinking how to pack one's goods safely but lightly, and wondering where other people get all that polystyrene, straw and tea-chests? For information on Packing Supplies, regulations and appropriate standards, ask PIRA, Randalls Road, Leatherhead, Surrey. Tel: 53 76161.

If your exports come under the heading of 'Fine-Art', then it can be wise to enlist the services of specialists in 'Fine-Art', then it can be wise to enlist the services of specialists in 'Fine-Art' packing, insurance and shipping, such as LEP Packing Limited, Corney Road, London, W4, or Pitt & Scott Ltd, 20 Eden Grove, London, N7.

All Legal and Above Board

Chapter Six
Statutory Regulations

CHAPTER SIX: Statutory Regulations

All Legal and Above Board

It is not possible, nor particularly desirable, to collect into one chapter all the statutory regulations which may be relevant to your enterprise. However, some basic regulations are of interest to almost all self-employed persons or new employers. I have concentrated particularly on those for people just starting up, and those on a low income.

Finances

National Insurance Contributions

When starting a business, even if whilst otherwise still employed, you should tell your local Inspector of Taxes whose address appears in the local Telephone Directory under 'Inland Revenue'. If you have left your previous employment, you should send him your P45 form.

NATIONAL INSURANCE CONTRIBUTIONS COME UNDER FOUR CLASSES

Class 1   Flat-rate contributions for employers and employees, paid when an employee is earning over a basic minimum wage. These contributions are earnings-related. It is the responsibility of the employer to deduct income tax and National Insurance Contributions under the Pay as You Earn scheme, from the wages of his employees. See leaflets P7, 'The Employer's Guide to PAYE', and NP15, 'Employers Guide to National Insurance Contributions'.

Class 2   Contributions payable if you are self-employed. These are at a fixed rate, and are slightly less for women than for men. They can be paid by direct debit from Bank or Giro Account to the DHSS, or by stamps stuck on a card. You may be excepted from paying these contributions if your earnings are too low. Further information from Leaflet N142.

Class 3   Voluntary contributions which can be paid in addition to class 1 or class 2 contributions under certain circumstances to help you to qualify for certain benefits. See Leaflet N1 42.

Class 4   Payable on demand from the Inland Revenue, collected with Schedule D Income Tax if your income exceeds a certain limit. See Leaflet N1 27A.
    Depending on your circumstances you may have to pay more than one of these contributions, but there is an upper yearly limit above which your contributions will be refunded.

War pensioners   In general, War Pensioners are obliged to pay NI contributions in the same way as anyone else, but, in the case of a War Pensioner who receives an Unemployability Supplement, he can still earn through self-employment a limited income (set each year) whilst still being exempt from paying class 2 contributions. See Leaflet NI 150.

Training for future employment It is possible for people undertaking a vocational, technical or rehabilitative course of training and who have been paying their National Insurance contributions in the normal way, to have these contributions credited to them without actually paying them, provided that the course is not intended to last more than a year (unless theirs is a course for disabled people under the Employment and Training Act). Courses pursued through the Manpower Services Commission entitle you automatically to have your credits recorded for the duration of the course, and no special applications are needed. If however, you attend other courses, you must apply for the credits yourself. You can obtain the necessary application CF55C form from your Local Social Security Office, see Leaflet NI 125.

NATIONAL INSURANCE CONTRIBUTIONS FOR CERTAIN MEMBERS OF THE EMPLOYMENT SECTOR

Company Directors Company Directors, as a general rule, pay class 1 contributions as an employee of the company, based on a percentage of all earnings within the specified limits in the same way as other employees. There are however, several aspects of statutory regulations which apply exclusively to Company Directors. For further information see Leaflet NI 35.

EXAMINERS, PART-TIME LECTURERS, TEACHERS AND INSTRUCTORS

Some part-time lecturers, teachers and instructors are engaged under a contract of service and as such are employees, liable to pay class 1 contributions. This generally applies to teaching regular classes (e.g. evening classes) in universities, schools and colleges, and not to private classes or individual tuition for which the tutor is paid directly by the student. A person engaged to give a series of public lectures at an educational establishment is not classed as an employee. See Leaflet NI 222.

NATIONAL INSURANCE BENEFITS

Some benefits to which you are entitled, depend upon your NI contributions:
Maternity Allowance (Leaflet NI 17a)
Unemployment Benefit (Leaflet NI 12)
Sickness Benefit (Leaflet NI 16)
Invalidity Benefit (Leaflet NI 210)
Retirement Pension (Leaflet NP 31)
    Some Benefits for married couples rely only upon the husband's contributions:

Maternity Grant
Widow's Benefits (Leaflet NI 13)
Child's Special Allowance (Leaflet NI 93)
Death Grant (Leaflet NI 49)
  Others are awarded without NI contributions:
Guardians Allowance (Leaflet NI 14)
Industrial Injuries Benefit (Leaflets NI 2, N15, N16)
Invalid Care Allowance (Leaflet NI 212)
Mobility Allowance (NI 211)
Family Allowances (Leaflet FAM 1)
Family Income Supplement (Leaflet FIS 1)
Supplementary Benefits (Leaflet SB 1)
Child Interim Benefit for One-Parent-Families (Leaflet CH 1B)

Help for Low Wage Earners

NATIONAL INSURANCE CONTRIBUTIONS FOR PEOPLE WITH LOW INCOMES FROM SELF-EMPLOYMENT

If your earnings are from a hobby or spare-time occupation, and are below a certain limit (approx £250 pa) then you do not have to bother with NI contributions.

If your self-employment is a little more serious, but still brings in only a low income (the upper limit of which is decided each year), then you are still not obliged to pay class 2 contributions, but you are expected to apply for a certificate of exemption each year. This is simply a matter of filling in Form CF10, part of Leaflet NI 27A, obtainable from the usual sources.

If however, you have been paying full contributions in the past, and feel that the present low income may not be a permanent state of affairs, you may if you wish, pay voluntary class 3 contributions to preserve your entitlement to the benefits which they provide.

Your right to exemption will be decided on your total *net* earnings after deductions have been made from gross earnings for allowable expenses. If you have more than one form of self-employment, then the net earnings of each must be added together, but a loss incurred in one may be off-set against a profit in another.

RATE REBATES

As long as you are not receiving supplementary benefit, owner-occupiers and tenants can claim a rebate on their general rates. The amount varies with the amount of your income, the amount of rates payable, and whether or not you live in London, as well as the number of your dependents.

More people are entitled to rent rebates than one would think. To check for yourself whether you are eligible, consult the table: 'Rent Rebates – Income Guide' in Leaflet FB1 Family Benefits and Pensions.

Rent Rebates

Most tenants, except those receiving Supplementary Benefit, who find it difficult to afford the full rent of their home, may apply to the local Authority for direct financial help. The amount of the rebate or allowance is governed by three main factors: the amount of your gross income, the size of your family, and the amount of rent payable. Again more people are entitled to this assistance, and it is more substantial, than many people think. Even a single person with no dependents, but living on a low income could find that they have to pay hardly any rent or rates at all. People with relatively high incomes may also be eligible for help.

For a general guide you could consult the table of 'Rent Rebates and Allowances – Income Guide' also in Leaflet FBI, but remember that the Local Authority will make the final decision as there are many factors which have to be taken into account.

Low Income Entitlements

Anyone over the age of 16 whose income is below a certain level, can obtain help with the cost of dental treatment, glasses, milk and vitamins, prescription charges and hospital fares. See Leaflets M11 and H11, both of which include a claim form.

Supplementary Benefits

If you are not in full-time employment, and are starting a business slowly, you may, for a time, need to supplement your earnings. Supplementary Benefits are awarded to those whose income is not enough to live on, and who do not qualify for other pensions or benefits. It is either a full pension for those who are unemployed and do not qualify for unemployment benefit, or for people in part-time employment who require a top-up payment. Receivers of Supplementary Benefit may also be entitled to free school meals, milk and vitamins, dental treatment etc. To find out more ask at your local Social Security Office or obtain the Leaflets mentioned from your local Citizens Advice Bureau.

Family Income Supplement

To apply for Family Income Supplement you must be in full-time employment (30 hrs or more a week), whether this be for an employer or on your own account. In the case of a couple it must be the man who is in full-time employment. You can claim FIS if your total income, which includes the gross income of you and your wife, is below the prescribed level for your size of family. The supplement equals half the difference between your total income and the prescribed minimum for your family. For a single-parent-family the benefit is the same. A self-employed person will be asked to send his latest profit and loss account. The claim will normally be dealt with by post in complete confidence.

65

LEGAL AID

Solicitors fees are normally high, so it is useful to know that if you are claiming Supplementary Benefit, or FIS, and you have a limited amount of disposable capital, then you are entitled to free legal aid. Otherwise, if your income is low, you only have to pay a contribution related to your earnings towards the legal costs. See 'Financial Conditions for Legal Aid' available from Citizens Advice Bureau, or the Central Office of Information, Hercules Road, London SE1 7DU.

General

INCOME TAX

There is no simple summing up of Income Tax Regulations, and the best person to advise you on this is a qualified accountant. However, there are several Guides and Leaflets for those of you who are determined to be independent, including 'Starting in Business' by the Inland Revenue, available from Her Majesty's Stationery Office, intended to give you an outline on how you will be assessed for tax on your profits, and of what records it is in your best interest to keep.

RETENTION OF CORRESPONDENCE AND RECORDS

If you are a Company, then Company Law requires that all records of financial transactions should be kept for seven years. Letters are usually kept for a similar period of time. Also, if by some mad chance you fail to send in your bills for seven years, then your debtors are no longer legally required to pay you.

AUDITED ACCOUNTS

You are legally obliged to have your Accounts audited only if you are a Limited Company, Charity or Co-operative.

Premises

Tenancy

There are no laws which insist that you hold a tenancy agreement or lease for any premises which you may rent. A letter from your landlord setting out terms of tenancy, to which you respond by a letter of acceptance, will suffice, but is not really satisfactory. In the event of a dispute between you and your landlord, loose terms of agreement can lead to far greater difficulties in settlement. For a modest fee, you solicitor can exchange with your prospective landlord formal letters of contract defining precisely what both parties promise to do for each other. In the case where there is an existing lease for the premises which you wish to occupy, the respective solicitors of you and your landlord must get together to make the legal arrangements for you to take over the lease under the agreed terms. This will involve you not only in solicitor's fees, but also in certain stamp duties as well, and should be budgeted for in advance.

Planning Permission

According to the Town and Country Planning Act, any external alteration to a building, even the addition of a sign, requires the approval of the Town Planning Officer.

His approval must also be obtained if you are planning a 'change of use' of what is scheduled as one type of accommodation, to another, i.e. living accommodation to office accommodation.

Planning permission is more important in a residential area than in a spacious rural area where hammering at midnight is unlikely to annoy the neighbours.

In the case where you are building a new workshop, then it is best to show your plans and drawings of the proposed building to the local planning department right from the start. If you fail to apply for planning permission, or if you ignore a condition or refusal of planning permission, you could be served with an enforcement notice ordering you to restore the building or land to its former state. Many buildings, especially older types, have a clause in the lease which prevent certain activities, such as manufacturing, taking place, so check your lease.

Further information can be found in 'A Comprehensive Guide to Town Planning Law and Procedures' by Robert McGown, published by George Godwin.

Safety

As usual, the law is not all that interested in how many risks you take with your own life, but it is interested if you become responsible for others, i.e. if you become an employer, or your workshop is open to the public. At least one month before you start a factory – defined as 'Any premises where people are employed to make things, to repair, alter or finish things, by way of trade or for purposes of gain' – you must contact HM Factory Inspectorate. Your District Inspector who is to be found in the Yellow Pages of the Telephone Directory, will come all prepared to discover potential hazards to life and limb in your premises, as will the Fire Officer. Most of their suggestions however, will be inspired by common sense. They will be interested in fire precautions, fire exits, ventilation, guarding dangerous machinery, overcrowding, temperature, lighting, wash-basins and toilets, and the provision of a first-aid box. It is as well to listen to their suggestions as, not only do they have the weight of the Factories Act behind them, but they may well save injuries, or the loss of your entire livelihood, or even loss of life.

The local Factory Inspectorate issue a free Leaflet, 'So you want to start a factory?' (SHW8)

Insurance

Again, you are not obliged to pay for any insurances except National Insurance, unless you become an employer, or your premises are open to the public. However, it would be extremely rash of you not to cover yourself for fire, theft, flooding, accident and sickness, as these disasters can befall any of us.

Every business is a unique case, and when seeking insurance, it is advisable to go to an insurance broker for advice. Their services are usually free as they receive a commission from the Insurance Company.

Most Insurance Companies offer a comprehensive policy for small businesses, a policy which combines all the risks under one cover and means that you pay only one premium. Otherwise, the areas you will need to cover by insurance are:

BUILDINGS
This includes damage or destruction caused by fire; lightning; explosion; earthquake; storm; flood and burst pipes; riot and malicious damage.

CONTENTS
The contents and stock of materials and goods of the premises should be insured against all the previously mentioned perils, as well as theft. Valuable items may have to be listed separately. The insurance company will insist that you make your premises and valuables as safe as possible by the provision of strong locks, safes and so on.

EMPLOYERS LIABILITY. (REQUIRED BY LAW)
If your employees are injured or become ill in the course of working for you, even if that work is part-time, you may be faced with a bill for damages of thousands of pounds. You must insure against this.

PUBLIC LIABILITY. (REQUIRED BY LAW)
If a member of the public is so stunned by the sight of your latest creation, that he trips and breaks his leg, then again you may have to pay damages. Also, if his property is lost or damaged whilst on your premises, you may have to pay up, and for both these risks you must be insured.

SICKNESS AND PERSONAL ACCIDENT
If you are the one with the broken leg, or recurrent malaria, the sight of mounting piles of bills and lost orders is not likely to make you feel better. Accident policies are generally included in one of the comprehensive schemes, but illness policies are high, particularly if you are not generally a healthy person.

LIFE AND ENDOWMENT ASSURANCES
In addition to the obvious considerations when taking out a life insurance, remember that the premium paid can be set against income tax, and the policy used as security when applying for a loan or overdraft.

PENSIONS
You can provide yourself with the security of knowing that your old age is going to be quite cosy, by taking out one of the self-employed pension policies, which are fairly flexible to allow for different earnings in each year, and are also tax deductible. General Accident is one of the Companies which issue such policies.

INSURANCE FOR JEWELLERS
Jewellers who deal in precious metals are notoriously at risk from burglars. One recommended company for jewellers is Halford Shead & Co Ltd, Halford House, Coral Lane, Chelmsford, Essex.

Remember, in these times of inflation, that it is not enough to take out an insurance policy at the start of your venture and then to tuck the policy away in a drawer and forget about it. Policies should be constantly updated to bring the amount for which you are covered into line with current prices and values.

Disabled Staff

If you have 20 or more staff you must employ a quota (3% at present) of registered people with disabilities. It is not against the law to be below quota, but people with disabilities must be considered for all vacancies until your quota is reached. The Disablement Reassessment Officer (DRO) can help you find suitable disabled workers, or, if none are available, will give you a permit to employ able-bodied people.

Of course, if you employ less than 20 people, but have work which you think may be suitable for a disabled person, you can make this known at any time to the Disablement Resettlement Officer who can be contacted through your local Employment Office or Job Centre.

HELP!

Is There Anybody There?

Chapter Seven

Advisory Organisations

CHAPTER SEVEN: Advisory Organisations

Help! Is There Anybody There?

There are probably more helpful organisations in existance than you think. In the last few years, especially, there has been a rising interest in the development of the small business sector of industry and commerce. The help that can be obtained from these organisations falls basically into two categories – financial assistance, and advice.

Financial Assistance

Clearing Banks

For most entrepreneurs the first funds come from personal savings, from the sale of unwanted possessions, gifts, private loans from friends and relatives, and personal or trade credit.

Often, in addition to your personal capital, an overdraft from a clearing bank such as Lloyds or the Midland Bank, is sought. This is one of the easiest, most flexible sources of loan capital, as long as you are able to provide some security, or are able to find a guarantor.

Clearing banks also provide medium term loans from one to five years. Capital and interest are repayable at regular intervals, but the interest on a loan is generally higher than on an overdraft. The bank will again require security, although this can sometimes be from guaranteed orders for your product or service. Security can also be in the form of your house, car, other valuables, or a life-insurance policy.

No bank will ever lend you all the money you need to start a business as, quite rightly, they expect you to risk some of your own capital to prove your commitment and confidence.

Clearing banks provide about half the new money for industry every year.

'Finance for Industry' – is owned by large banks, including a 15% share by the Bank of England. They were Government-sponsored to lend £1,000m in 1975 and 1976. These loans are usually medium sized (over £5,000) repayable over ten years or less.

'FFI', 7 Coptall Avenue, London EC2R 7DD.

Government Funds

The general rule with Government money is that the further West and North you go, the cheaper and more plentiful it becomes. However, this does not mean that if you live in East Anglia, or London, you do not stand a chance of being helped.

72

THE DEPARTMENT OF INDUSTRY
The Dept of Industry is empowered to give Regional Development grants to what they call 'assisted areas'. Assisted areas are divided into three categories: Intermediate Areas, Development Areas, and Special Development Areas, and the scale of the grants available vary according to which type of area you qualify for. Most assisted areas are in the North and North West of Britain including Wales and Scotland.

They now concentrate mainly on manufacturing industries, but this term includes all manner of products including weaving, lace-making, toys and games, pottery etc. Grants are for machinery or plant, and buildings and works. If you wish to know if you might qualify for a grant, the Department of Industry issues two documents, RDG/PEN (machinery or plant) and RDG/BEN (buildings and works) which are a brave, if hopeless, attempt at explaining the grants system clearly.

For further information write to the Regional Development Grants Division, The Dept of Industry, Millbank, SW1. They have regional offices in Cleveland, Merseyside, Cardiff and Glasgow.

GRANTS TO SMALL INDUSTRIES
ENGLAND: CoSIRA (Council for Small Industries in Rural Areas)
If you employ less than twenty people, and live in a town of up to 10,000 inhabitants, then you are eligible for assistance from CoSIRA.

CoSIRA was set up by the Development Commission in 1968 to bring together three separate units – The Rural Industries Bureau, The Rural Industries Loan Fund Ltd, and the County Organisers formerly employed by the Rural Community Councils. They are financed by the Development Commission and they are responsible for providing advice and loans to help small manufacturing and servicing industries in the rural areas of England and Wales to become more prosperous. They also assist enterprises designed to attract tourists to certain rural areas designated as Development Areas.

Loans are available to eligible businesses to assist with the financing of buildings and/or equipment and/or working capital. A loan may be up to 80% of the cost of the project, reaching a maximum of £50,000 at any one time (1979). Repayment may be made between two and twenty years according to the type of loan. They usually assist established workshops, however small, to get bigger. They do not usually invest money in completely new ventures, although they do provide much advice and expertise for the beginner, (see Advisory Organisations).

CoSIRA also administers the Vaughan Nash Memorial Trust which provides small grants for craftsmen or their apprentices in rural areas, to buy tools, or to help pay for educational courses connected with their craft. Grants are mainly awarded to young people.

To make an enquiry to CoSIRA, the first step is to contact your local

Organiser whose name and address is available on request from their registered office, Queens House, Fish Row, Salisbury, Wilts, SP1 1EX.

SCOTLAND: SICRAS (Small Industries Council for Rural Areas of Scotland) This is the Scottish equivalent of CoSIRA, and enjoys similar powers. In the last few years SICRAS has laid emphasis on crafts, and has initiated several special schemes including a Crafts Entrants Scheme, a Craftsmen's Grants Scheme and an Apprenticeship Scheme.
SICRAS, 27 Walker Street, Edinburgh, Scotland.

HIDB (Highlands and Islands Development Board)
In the same way as CoSIRA and SICRAS, the HIDB promotes cottage industries in Northern Scotland, recognising that these industries are particularly suitable for people living in remote areas. Generally speaking, successful applicants can expect to receive up to 50% of the costs of their project from public funds (HIDB and the Department of Industry).
HIDB have recently taken an initiative by appointing two young field officers to pioneer 'Multi-Functional Co-Operatives' in the Outer Hebrides. They will encourage the formation of Co-Operative Steering Committees which will usually be offshoots of Community Associations, and they will advise on the feasibility of projects. The aim is to create an enterprise which will administer a variety of different projects which are appropriate to the resources of the local community. An essential element will be the raising of funds locally. These will be supplemented by the Development Board, who will also cover the cost of a Co-Operative Manager for the first three years.
HIDB, Bridge House, 27 Bank Street, Inverness, Scotland.
The Scottish Development Agency, Small Business Division, are also worth approaching for advice and assistance. They are at 102 Telford Road, Edinburgh EH4 2NP.

NORTHERN IRELAND: LEDU (Local Enterprise Development Unit)
The Northern Ireland equivalent of CoSIRA and SICRAS. They are also empowered to give grants for the establishment of new craftsmen, capital grants for workshops, equipment, employment grants and bursaries.
LEDU, 21 Linehall Street, Belfast 2, Northern Ireland.

WALES Contact the Welsh Development Agency, Small Business Division, Treforest Industrial Estate, Pontypridd, CF37 5UT, Mid Glams.

Crafts Advisory Committee (CAC) and Joint Crafts Committee (JCC)

CAC promotes high quality craftsmanship throughout England and Wales. JCC is the Scottish equivalent. They make grants and loans to craftsmen working individually or in groups. To apply you will have to show examples of your work and also provide the Committee with a written account of your past, present and future, in relation to the craft you have chosen. Grants and loans available include:

NEW CRAFTSMEN GRANT:
About 150 – 200 craftsmen a year are given this grant to help set up a first workshop.

MAINTENANCE GRANT:
Awarded primarily on the quality of the work of the applicant, this grant is usually for a year to help supplement a low income whilst becoming established. It may be awarded together with the New Craftsmen's Grant.

TRAINING GRANT:
This is paid to Master Craftsmen to take on art college graduates or untrained apprentices. Grants are paid at different rates for each category of trainee.

SPECIAL PROJECTS GRANT:
This is an unrestricted grant, usually given to a group of people for one-off projects which are not easily classifiable.

BURSARY SCHEME:
For established craftsmen, this is a grant which enables one to undertake a project which is purely creative, and probably totally uneconomical. It is only awarded in special cases.

LOANS:
Intended primarily for established craftsmen with their own workshop, they are mainly for equipment and materials. The loans are for a period of five years, repayable at 10% interest at regular monthly intervals. If all the repayments are made satisfactorily, the whole of the interest will be awarded in the form of a grant.

The address of the Crafts Advisory Committee is 12 Waterloo Place, London SW1. The Joint Crafts Committee is at the Scottish Economic Planning Department, St Andrew's House, Edinburgh, Scotland.

The National Research Development Corporation

If you have some capital, and the know-how to set up a company of your own, but are completely at a loss to know what the company should produce, then it may interest you to know that it is possible to license other people's innovative ideas, and receive supplementary financial backing under a 'Development Contract' to manufacture the particular design.

The National Research and Development Corporation was set up by Parliament in 1949 primarily to encourage more effective exploitation of inventive ideas arising in the United Kingdom and, through the licensing of Patents and know-how, to maximise the national benefit.

The scheme works firstly by the careful vetting of well thought out, innovative ideas which are aimed at a genuine advance in technology; and secondly, by establishing that the 'client' firm to whom they will license the design, is suitable both financially and technically to undertake the task with a reasonable chance of success.

The NRDC shares the cost of the project with the accepted company on an individual 'tailor-made' basis. Advances to the company are made monthly or quarterly against invoices relating to the agreed percentage (which can be 50% or more of the expenditure on an approved programme of work). Recovery of NRDC funds is from levies, imposed from an agreed date, upon the proceeds from commercial sales, or usage, of the particular process or service(s), at a level which, in the event of success will give NRDC the return of its capital with fair premium related to the risks inherent in the project. The cost to the company is related to the success of the venture supported. Advances and levy repayments are outside the scope of VAT legislation.

The Corporation, which is financed by loans from the Department of Industry, is not a Government Department, but a commercial organisation which expects to receive a fair return on investments.

Further details may be obtained from the Commercial Services Controller, Industrial Development Office, National Research and Development Corporation, Kingsgate House, 66-74 Victoria Street, London SW1 6SL. Tel: 01.828 3400.

Local Authorities

Many assist small firms and some have set up separate organisations for this purpose, e.g. The Greater Manchester Economic Development Association, and the Staffordshire Development Association.

ICOF (Industrial Common Ownership Finance Limited)

This is a revolving loan fund administered by ICOM (see Chapter 3, 'Co-operatives') to help firms change to Common Ownership. They are also now responsible for the application of Government Funds under the Industrial Common Ownership Bill, made available to promote the development of Co-operatives.

Further details are available from Industrial Common Ownership Finance Limited, 1 Gold Street, Northampton NN1 1SA. Tel: 0604 37563.

Grants for Disabled People

Under section 15 of the Disabled Persons' (Employment) Act 1944, the Manpower Services Commission are empowered to give grants to enable severely disabled people to work on their own account, if no other possible employment can be found, and where the proposed business appears to be a viable proposition.

Aids to employment, eg braille micrometers, adapted typewriters, sewing machines etc, may also be supplied by the Employment Service Agency on permanent loan.

Application for help under these schemes should be made in the first place through your local Disablement Resettlement Officer.

GLAID

GLAID stands for the Greater London Association for Initiatives in Disablement. It is a charitable Association set up by a small group of people, most of whom are themselves disabled, and who wish to assist people with disabilities to have greater control over their own lives.

They have set up a small grant/loan giving Fund to promote promising projects initiated by people with disabilities, particularly in the field of employment. Grants are for capital expenditure only. Loans are interest-free and are made to potentially profit-making, or self-perpetuating projects, for starter finance or development costs. A 5% service fee is charged on loans. Repayment terms are negotiatable.

GLAID will also help applicants to raise finances from other sources, or apply on their behalf where this is appropriate.

In addition to financial assistance, GLAID is building up a pool of information for disabled people who are starting such a venture, which includes the resources of specialist advisers such as an adviser on individual electronic aids for employment purposes.

Apply to The Secretary, GLAID, Flat 4, 188 Ramsden Road, Balham, London SW12. 01.673 4310.

Charitable Trusts and Foundations

Even if you are not a registered charity, it is sometimes possible to obtain funds from Trusts and Foundations if the objects of your project are to promote either the Arts, Crafts, Education, Religion, Social Health and Welfare, Preservation of Buildings, Research, or one of several other categories.

'A Directory of Grant Making Trusts', published by the Charities Aid Fund, is available at Public Reference Libraries, or from the National Council of Social Service, 26 Bedford Square, London WC1. This Directory lists most Trusts, their aims, objects and restrictions. If you think you might be considered by one of these Trusts for a grant, then you can write to them and put your case. You lose nothing, and it might just be your lucky day.

For a list of educational charities, write to the National Union of Students, 3 Endsleigh Street, London WC1.

Advisory Organisations

Small Firms Service

Small Firms Information Centres can be found at:

SCOTLAND	57 Bothwell Street, Glasgow G2 6TU	041 248 6014 Freefone 846
WALES	16 St David's House, Wood Street, Cardiff CF1 1ER	Cardiff 396116 Freefone 1208
NORTHERN REGION	22 Newgate Shopping Centre, Newcastle-upon-Tyne NE1 5RH	Newcastle 25353 Freefone 6005
NORTH-WEST REGION	Peter House, Oxford Street, Manchester M1 5AN	061 832 5282 Freefone 6005
(Sub-Office for Liverpool)	1 Old Hall Street, Liverpool L3 9HJ	051 236 5756
YORKSHIRE AND HUMBERSIDE REGION	1 Park Row, City Square, Leeds LS1 5NR	Leeds 445151 Freefone 5361
EAST MIDLANDS REGION	48-50 Maid Marion Way, Nottingham NG1 6GF	Nottingham 49791 Freefone 4062
WEST MIDLANDS REGION	53 Stephenson Street, Birmingham B2 4DH	021643 3344 Freefone 4054
EASTERN REGION	35 Wellington Street, Luton W1 2SB	Luton 29215 Freefone 372
LONDON AND SOUTH EASTERN REGION	35 Buckingham Palace Road, London SW1W 0QX	01 828 2384 Freefone 2079
SOUTH WEST REGION	Colston Centre, Colston Avenue, Bristol BS1 4UB	Bristol 294 546 Freefone 9910

A similar service is provided in Northern Ireland by the Department of Commerce. Freefone is a free telephone service. Dial the operator and ask for Freefone, followed by the appropriate number.

The Scottish Council

The Scottish Council (Development and Industry) was formed in 1946. It is financed voluntarily by local authorities, companies, banks, chambers of commerce, trade unions and other corporate bodies as well as by private individuals, all of whom are represented on the Executive Committee, which is the governing body.

The broad aim of the Council is to promote the industrial and social development of Scotland, so that anyone who wishes to live and work in Scotland should be able to do so, whatever his employment or profession. They research carefully the current economic conditions and prospects of Scotland, and formulate policies based on this information, lobbying publicly and privately for their acceptance by Government and public agencies. They work directly with companies in Scotland and abroad through their programme of trade missions and information services. They issue several publications including 'Business Prospects' which lists available licences and joint ventures; diary dates including trade and craft fairs, exhibitions and conferences; sub contractors in Scotland, and import/export opportunities.

Their head office is at 1 Castle Street, Edinburgh EH2 3AJ. They also have offices in Glasgow, Aberdeen, Inverness and London.

(See also 'Financial Assistance' above)

All these organisations give advice, and sometimes technical assistance to small firms, even those consisting of one person.

CoSIRA, for example, employs many local organisers all over England and Wales with whom you can get in touch. CoSIRA gives technical and managerial advice on a wide range of subjects including estimating, marketing, costing, workshop design and layout, all at a very modest fee. They sometimes organise Exhibitions and Fairs to help publicise and sell the work of local entrepreneurs.

They issue several publications including 'Craft Workshops in the Countryside', a handbook for tourists and others interested in visiting small workshops where British crafts are produced. If your standard of work is acceptable, and you are prepared for visitors, you can advertise yourself in the handbook to attract new customers.

CoSIRA Advisory Services, 35 Camp Road, Wimbledon Common, London SW19 4UP. Tel: 01.947 6761.

Enterprise North

Enterprise North is a voluntary organization working through New Enterprise Panels in seven areas in the North East and Cumbria. Each panel is made up of businessmen with years of experience in the financial, technical and marketing fields, whose sole aim is to help establish successful business ventures in the North. The panel will consider the plans you have for a business in detail, and will give advice on the viability of the idea, how to start, possible improvements to your product or your marketing and selling ideas. They may be able to give advice on finding a partner, alternative sources of funding, or in the construction of a comprehensive business plan. The services of Enterprise North are free and confidential.

To contact Enterprise North ring or write to: The Co-Ordinating Centre, Enterprise North, Durham University Business School, Mill Hill Lane, Durham DH1 3LB. Tel: Durham 41919 Ext 42.

London Enterprise Agency (LENTA)

The London Enterprise Agency began operating in April 1979. It is sponsored by nine major companies including Barclays Bank Ltd, BOC Ltd, The British Petroleum Company Ltd, GEC Ltd, IBM United Kingdom Ltd, Industrial and Commercial Finance Corporation Ltd, Marks and Spencer Ltd, Midland Bank Ltd, and Shell UK Ltd. It is the result of a growing sense of responsibility within the private sector of industry for the rest of the community. Their aims are:

(a) to provide help and assistance for both new and existing firms.

(b) to develop small firms' estates with central services. The first such project will be a 2 acre estate in Wandsworth provided by Shell UK Ltd

(c) to bring together people who need each other, e.g. private investors with small firms, and entrepreneurs with complementary skills

(d) to help people to present effective cases to possible sources of funds

(e) to assist the aleviation of institutionalised constraints upon small firms by spotlighting obvious difficulties; undertaking research to spotlight less obvious difficulties; and making representations on behalf of small firms to government, politicians and other policy makers.

(f) to assist the regeneration of the inner city of London.

The agency is set up under the auspices of the London Chamber of Commerce and Industry at 69 Cannon Street, London EC4N 5AB. Tel: 01.236 2676/77 or 01.248 4444.

Smaller Business Association

This association aims to further the proposition that 'the best long-term interests of British Industry are best served by a virile and thrusting small business sector'. Services provided include assistance with raising capital, import/export problems, and international contacts. The Smaller Business Association, Europe House, World Trade Centre, London E1. Tel: 01.481 8669.

The Institute of Small Business

Ideas and advice on business opportunities. The Institute of Small Business, Tower Suite, 1 Whitehall Place, London SW1. Tel: 01.930 4001.

Citizens' Advice Bureaux

A wealth of information is available for the asking at your local Bureau. Here is the place to go if you need information on benefits, National Insurance, legal problems, local contacts, other advisory organisations, and much else. Many bureaux employ professional advisers with whom you can make an appointment, including accountants and solicitors, many of whom have a special interest in the small businessman.

Addresses and telephone numbers are in your local Telephone Directory.

Local Enterprise Trusts

A recent development in the mobilisation of local support is the formation of several Local Enterprise Trusts.

At a weekend workshop, at which many of the pioneers of these Trusts met with others who were still contemplating the formation of a LET in their own locality, this definition of a LET was agreed: 'A Local Enterprise Trust is a broadly based local group involved in the creation of worthwhile work through the fostering and development of small-scale enterprises.

It functions primarily by helping with access to technical and professional assistance and information, and by promoting collaborative arrangements as in, for example, marketing and the provision of premises.

It is a non-profit organisation which may (or may not) establish trading subsidiaries in pursuit of its primary ends'.

Further information can be obtained from: The Association of Local Enterprise Trusts, John Davis, Wilton Corner, 10 Grenfell Road, Beaconsfield, Bucks. Tel: Beaconsfield 3080.

Action Resource Centre

Action Resource Centre was formed to encourage industry and commerce to help the community. If your project is of social value, e.g. helping unemployed young people, or disabled people, or is a voluntary organisation and needs skilled assistance, Action Resource Centre will try to find business employees who may be seconded on a part-time or full-time basis, to work with you, and to provide the expertise you may lack, and would not otherwise be able to afford.

Action Resource Centre, 7 Strutton Ground, London SW1 Tel: 01.222 2922.

Crafts Advisory Committee (CAC)

Apart from the grants, loans and bursaries outlined above under 'Financial Assistance', CAC exists to promote British craftsmen through exhibitions; as an information service, and as an index of craftsmen. They publish 'Crafts', a bi-monthly mgazine for craftsmen.

Crafts Advisory Committee, 12 Waterloo Place, London SW1.

Craft Guilds and Associations

CAC is the central body from which many national and local craft guilds and associations are promoted. They issue a list of both national and local craft societies in England and Wales, (reference list 5), including:-

THE BRITISH TOYMAKERS GUILD
The guild was formed in 1956 by a group of Toymakers who were convinced that active steps should be taken to encourage the production of better quality, well designed toys.

81

Among its services the Guild offers guidance on marketing, and where possible, on technical and production problems. The Guild also promotes periodic exhibitions in public halls and stores at which members may display the items which have received the Guilds emblem of approval. New members are immediately included in the membership list. This list, constantly updated, gives details of members products and goes out to everyone in the Guild. Members are thus put in contact with others in the toymaking field, to the mutual advantage of all. In addition, the Guild provides members with up-to-date lists of suppliers of soft-toy, and wooden-toy materials, and also names of retailers who are sympathetic to the Guilds' ideals. Further information is available from: The Secretary, British Toymakers Guild Centre, 32-34 The Ridgeway, London SW19.

SOCIETY OF DESIGNER CRAFTSMEN
This aims to : 'promote creative craftmanship in Britain and to bring a professional standard of individual craftmanship to bear on the enrichment of domestic and civic environment'.

The activities of this society include exhibitions, annual conferences and the donation of the Marlow Award for work of outstanding excellence. Annual membership fees vary for different types of membership, including Student, Licentiate, Associate, Ordinary and Fellow. Society of Designer Craftsmen, 43 Earlham Street, London WC2 H9LD.

GUILD OF SUSSEX CRAFTSMEN
This aims to 'encourage good craftsmanship, to create venues enabling craftsmen to sell direct to the public, to act as an agency in bringing the public's attention to the work of the craftsmen, and to encourage mutual aid'. There is a choice of full or associate membership. Secretary: Doreen Turner, 2 Spring Cottages, Peelings Lane, Westham, Pevensey, Sussex.

GUILDS TO PROMOTE ONE PARTICULAR CRAFT
There are also a host of guilds which promote one particular craft, the addresses of these can also be obtained from CAC, for example:

The Lace Society of Wales: This aims to keep lace-making alive and to encourage its practice.
Contact: Mrs P Kemp-Jones, Belvedere, Bradley, NrWrexham, Clwyd.

Basketmakers Association: To promote good design and workmanship in Basketry.
Contact: Mrs J Viall, Bieston House, Dean Way, Chalfont St Giles, Bucks.

Craftsmen Potters Association: This aims to encourage creative ceramics, to co-operate to sell work, and to increase informed opinion by the public.
Contact: William Blake House, Marshall Street, London W1.

Artist Enamellers: They encourage and promote good design and workmanship in enamel.
Contact: Richard Dent, 15 Moreton Place, London SW1.

Trade Associations

For most Crafts, Trades and Professions there are specific Trade Associations which provide information about new techniques, materials, specialised tools and much else. Addresses generally can be found in appropriate trade magazines. They are of course numerous, but include:

THE JEWELLERY INFORMATION CENTRE:
Mitre House, 44-46 Fleet St, London EC4. Official Information Centre for the Jewellery and Allied Industries.

EARLY MUSICAL INSTRUMENT MAKERS:
c/o Arnold Dolmetsch Ltd, Kings Road, Haslemere, Surrey. 'A trade association for professional musical instrument makers, and to improve standards'.

BRITISH PLASTICS FEDERATION:
47 Piccadilly, London W1. The trade association for the plastics industry which acts as an information bureau.

SMALL POTTERIES TRADE ASSOCIATION:
Ann Whalley, Haroldstone House, Clay Lane, Haverfordwest, Dyfed, Wales. Aims to 'promote the commercial interests of the members of the Association by providing mutual facilities for bulk purchasing and transport, arranging and manning group stands at exhibitions at home and abroad, providing a pool of information regarding suppliers, materials and retailers, and exploring the possibilities of export'.

Legal Structures – Centres for Advice and Registration

CHARITIES
For advice to any group wishing to become a Charity, write to The National Council of Social Service, 26 Bedford Square, London WC1. 01.636 4066.

For registration write to: The Charity Commission, 14 Ryder Street, London SW1. They publish 'Central Register of Charities, Leaflet RE4' for general information on the procedures of registration, and 'The Charity Commission, How They Can Help Charity Trustees'.

Applications for charitable registration in Scotland should be sent to: The Secretary of State for Scotland, Scottish Home and Health Department, St Andrew's House, Edinburgh, Scotland.

CO-OPERATIVES
For advice and information write to ICOM, 31 Hare Street, Woolwich, London.
For registration: The Registrar of Friendly Societies, 17 North Audley Street, London W1Y 2AP.

COMPANIES
For information purposes, the Companies Registration Office issue two useful leaflets – 'Incorporation of New Companies – Notes for Guidance', and 'Notes for the Guidance of Registered Companies'.
For registration write to: The Registrar of Companies, Companies Registration Office, Crown Way, Maindy, Cardiff, CF4 3UZ.

BUSINESSES & PARTNERSHIPS
For registration in England and Wales write to: The Registrar of Business Names, Companies House, 55-71 City Road, London EC1.
For registration in Scotland write to: The Registrar of Business Names, 102 George Street, Edinburgh, Scotland.

Miscellaneous Organisations
THE FRANCHISE ADVISORY CENTRE, 32 Stockwell Park Crescent, London SW9. They offer advice on how to obtain a franchise.

THE NATIONAL FEDERATION OF THE SELF-EMPLOYED, 32 St Anne's-on-Sea, Lancs. The Federation now represents over 50,000 self-employed and small-business people. They protest against 'discriminatory and pernicious legislation, penal and confiscatory taxation, imposed without regard for justice and the basic right of freedom'.

THE FORUM OF PRIVATE BUSINESS LTD
The Forum is a non partisan political pressure group whose object is to promote and preserve free competitive enterprise in this country by giving private business and professional people a greater voice in the legislation that affects all their businesses. The forum is a company limited by guarantee as a non-profit making organisation.
Their objectives are achieved by a system which provides members with information about forthcoming Bills and Issues to be considered by Parliament, and a central collection of votes of members relating to these issues, which are then presented to all elected members of the House of Commons, a select number of the House of Lords, and civil servants. This way all those who are involved in decision-making on behalf of private business are told how the members feel before they vote.

The Forum of Private Business Limited, Ruskin Rooms, Drury Lane, Knutsford, Cheshire WA16 0ED. Tel: Knutsford 4467/8.

AGRICULTURAL DEVELOPMENT AND ADVISORY SERVICE, Great Westminster House, Horseferry Road, London SW1, has about 30 regional offices giving free advice of a technical and scientific nature to agriculturalists.

INSTITUTE OF LINGUISTS, 91 Newington Causeway, London SE1. An information service for technical and commercial linguists.

ADVISORY CENTRE FOR EDUCATION, 32 Trumpington Street, Cambridge. An information service on all aspects of education. This publishes 'Where'.

The Proof
of the Pudding

CHAPTER EIGHT: Successful projects

The Proof of the Pudding

You will have noticed here and there, trapped between lumps of heavy text laden with facts, stories of people who coloured and enlivened the research for this book. They are the people who convinced me that my eternally optimistic belief in the ingenuity of mankind was founded in truth. This chapter contains a few more examples to illustrate the variety of ideas which have been made to succeed.

Dorothy Atree – Catering

Dorothy is a mother of school-age children who wanted to find work she could do from home. She had always enjoyed cooking and had taken pleasure in experimenting with recipes. One of her specialities was a 3-layer gateau, once eaten, never forgotten!

People knew of her interest and skill in cooking, and when family weddings and other special occasions arose, Dorothy was asked to do the catering. Those who attended these functions were so impressed by her ability that they recommended her services to their friends. Gradually Dorothy realised that this could be the opportunity which she was looking for to earn some money.

As a guide to prospective clients, she made a list of all the dishes she could do well and economically, and worked out a price per head. When the client had given her the go-ahead on any particular menu, she would buy all the foodstuffs and prepare everything in her small kitchen. The prepared food was then stored in an old refrigerator in their garage.

On the day of the event she would hire all the plates, cups, glasses, cutlery etc that were necessary, and also, if the event were of the nature at which food had to be served, she would hire waiters and waitresses. At the appropriate time she would deliver all the food and utensils, set them out, serve the guests, and clear up afterwards. Sometimes her husband would accompany her as barman.

Dorothy is considering taking on a partner to expand her service. She feels there is great potential in the project, both financially and pleasurewise, as long as late nights and a cluttered kitchen are acceptable to all those who have to live with it.

Talfryn Toys

Down a bumpity lane in the middle of Wiltshire, I found the farmhouse which is the home of a family business called Talfryn Toys.

The business originated several years ago when the father of the household, being an enthusiastic supporter of the British Legion, whipped-up the whole family to contribute their various talents to a British Legion exhibition of crafts. The work of Mrs Tolfree and her daughter Eleanor, which included little felt mice made into a mobile, was seen at the exhibition by a member of the local Crafts Association, who invited them to participate in more exhibitions.

At first the selling of toys was a hobby which brought in a little extra money at Christmas. However, a year ago, Eleanor found that the nursing career she had always planned to follow, was cut short by the sudden onset of epilepsy.

Until such time as her condition is stabilised, Eleanor has to reconsider ways to put her love of people and children in particular, as well as her other skills, to use within the confines of her disability.

The toymaking has consequently been developed into a home industry employing mother and daughter. Eleanor's speciality is designing toys which are based on realistic animals such as guinea-pigs, hedgehogs, zebras and bear cubs. They use off-cuts of fur fabrics, keeping an eye open for damaged or badly dyed pieces which can be adapted for use in novel ways. They use terylene filling and safety-lock eyes. Mrs Tolfree also knits and crochets, using rug wools 'off the cone' from a carpet factory. It is these cheaply bought materials which make their work economically viable.

They sell their work at exhibitions and through shops and private orders. Harrod's have offered to sell their work, but at the time of our interview, they did not feel able to cope with the large orders this would entail. Eleanor also does voluntary work three mornings a week in the psychotic and autistic unit of a school for mentally handicapped children, which she says she enjoys as much as she would have enjoyed nursing. One way in which she trys to make contact with these severely withdrawn children, is to play music to them on the clarinet and flute.

From Eleanor's story it is clear that one's work can involve a whole range of seemingly unconnected skills and interests which form a balance between practical skills, creativity and caring for other people, which may not be a financial bonanza, but which satisfy many of our basic human needs in terms of self-expression.

Vine – Hand Printed and Dyed Fabrics

This business was started by Helen Vine in a spare bedroom in her home. She and her husband both had some experience of learning textile dying and printing whilst undertaking a teacher-training course in London. Richard Vine took a job in open industry and supported Helen for a while during the initial stages of their venture. Helen sold her work through exhibitions, trade fairs and craft markets, as well as shops which she approached on selling trips.

When the business had built up sufficiently, Richard left his job to work with Helen. They now have a workshop of 36' × 24', and employ five outworkers to do the sewing and finishing.

They screen-print, or batik-print fabrics of cotton, silk or cotton/wool mixtures. The fabrics are sometimes made up into garments such as smocks or dresses, otherwise they are sold by the metre.

The advantage of running their own business is, they say, the ability to produce something they enjoy making within their own timetable. They admit however, that their flexibility is somewhat limited by the demands of their customers, and the necessity of producing something quickly and economically, and of a design that can be repeated. They feel they would like to have more time to experiment and explore new techniques. However, in their own words they 'still get a big kick from finding people who are sufficiently interested in their work to actually buy it'.

Mary Potter – Batik Artist

For the most part I have avoided exceptionally brilliant people in this book, as I believe that rubbing one's nose in the breath-taking talents of others generally encourages one to curl up in a corner with a good book in a defeated sort of pile, instead of inspiring one to have a go oneself. However, I have made an exception of Mary Potter because her craft of batik is still so rarely practised in Britain. This craft is so beautiful and has so many different applications that its scope needs to be explored and developed by many more enthusiastic people who like to work with textiles.

Batik is an ancient craft originating in Indonesia. Part of a design is painted onto cloth with hot wax, then the whole cloth is immersed in a cold-water dye. The process is repeated for each colour in the design. The wax cracks causing the characteristic 'marble' effect. Finally the wax is ironed out between layers of absorbent paper, leaving the finished design.

Mary Potter was born and raised on a Sussex farm. She went to art college where she completed a general course. It was not until considerably later however, after the War and the raising of three children, that she resumed her interest in art by taking further training at evening classes.

A few years ago there was little interest in arts and crafts as a serious subject in this country, consequently selling her work and building up a name was a slow affair.

Mary started mainly by printing silk-screen cards and scarves, later concentrating on batik which she found more creative and flexible. Her original studio was her kitchen, but now a large, light room in their house displays her work all over the walls, leaving plenty of space on the floor to spread the batiks to dry.

Mary is an artist as well as a craftsman, and has explored the scope of her craft, resulting in a highly individualist style. She works full-time, and her original designs, mostly based on the Sussex countryside, command prices equal to many respected contemporary painters.

Silk and cotton are the only fabrics suitable for batik. Mary has silk scarves for sale printed by both batik and silk-screen. The scarves she buys in bulk from a wholesaler in London and sells abroad.

There are good books on the subject of batik for those interested in developing the craft. One is called 'Batik for Beginners' by Norma Jameson, and is published by Studio Vista Publications, Blue Star House, Highgate Hill, London N19.

Libby Calvert — Patchwork

For Libby it all started with a Victorian patchwork bedspread which belonged to her great aunt. Libby's mother copied the bedspread, and Libby took the idea from her mother, but developing the use of colour in the design of the patchwork. She uses matching and blending cotton prints and sews the patchwork on a sewing machine instead of by hand.

This she pursued as a hobby for several years, making cushions and bedspreads for friends. Naturally she improved her standard and her speed all the time.

Finally, through friends, Libby had articles written about her in several leading newspapers and magazines, which brought in orders for her work from as far afield as Toronto and the Cayman Islands, as well as many in England. Her cushions are filled with feathers bought in 50 lb sacks. She enlists the aid of her children to fill the cushions, and they have had many hilarious moments in the process. Smaller cushions are scented with fragrantly scented pot pourri, also bought in bulk.

Libby works by herself, claiming to be far too erratic to work with anyone else. She hates the routine of nine-to-five jobs, and dreads the idea of being a secretary as she had been in the past. She likes being at home, and, although her work is really more than full-time, she manages to ease off in the school holidays to spend more time with her children. Libby also runs the crafts side of the West Oxfordshire Arts Association.

A. J. Martin — The Glass Workshop

Glass animals are made from coloured rods of glass heated over a butane burner and modelled whilst still in a molten state. It is one of the crafts which looks reasonably easy until you try it yourself.

A. J. Martin apprenticed for five years with a glass firm, and began to market his animals, trees and flowers whilst still in full-time employment.

At the time there was a 55% purchase tax charged on his particular goods which made it necessary for him to limit his turnover to £500 per annum which was the level of exemption from the purchase tax. Had he not done this the glass pieces he made would have been too expensive for people to buy. However, when VAT came into being, it became much more advantageous to earn more. Consequently, he became a full-time modeller. A loan in 1969 helped him to equip his tiny workshop and to buy materials. He sells his work by demonstrating to clubs of various sorts, and at shows, as well as selling through a few shops. He is full self-supporting, and says he enjoys not having to listen to people making critical or cynical remarks whilst he works.

91

'Impi'

This partnership is to be found by visitors of great determination in a tiny, garage-sized workshop, behind a house, behind a farm, near a little village in Wiltshire.

The workshop was built by Hedley Holgate, the originator of 'Impi', at a point in his life when he had nothing to do. He had retired from the army, started one business which floundered causing him to lose almost everything he had.

As he had always liked woodwork as a hobby, he made some dolls' house furniture for fun, and discovered some shops, including 'Minutiques' in Brighton, which were interested in buying them. For four years he 'pottered around' making miniature period furniture copied from photographs, working out all the time the best ways to make them, and also from where to get the accessories such as brass door-handles and hinges.

Eventually he decided he was fed up with working on his own all day, so he asked a friend to join him. Together they injected the business with both more machinery and enthusiasm, working almost seven days a week without becoming bored. To make the business profitable they have to make quite a lot of furniture, so they carefully plan together their week's schedule each Monday morning, spending a good deal of time inventing ways of producing several copies of the same thing efficiently.

Their market seems to fall into two categories – the simpler, faster doll's house furniture for England, and high quality scale period furniture for export to North America and Canada.

They collaborate with two other craftsmen, one who makes brass accessories, and the other who does the veneering. They employ three outworkers who do the sandpapering, staining and french polishing. They are hoping to expand their range to include upholstered furniture which will involve more outworkers.

The advantage of miniature work, they pointed out, is that one needs a small amount of space, small plant, and a small outlay in materials. Also miniatures are comparatively cheap and easy to transport. Hedley finished by saying 'I don't go out much, because I get so bored – I'm only really happy when I'm in my workshop'.

Nancy Willis – The Studio

Many people who choose as their main occupation to follow an art or craft, or other creative interest, often have quite a struggle to draw a balance between the need to be with other people, and the need for solitude. Nancy discovered this difficulty after leaving college with a Dip. AD in Fine Art, and trying to organise her life so that the various needs, complicated by the additional fact that she suffers from Muscular Dystrophy, were brought together in such a way that she could function as a whole person. It took quite a long time.

Firstly, through contacts made whilst doing a thesis on gypsies, she spent a summer teaching gypsy children. When the children finally enrolled in a State school, she began a two year period of working alone, completing major projects including a large wall mural, the execution of which involved balancing her wheelchair on tables and bricks and all sorts of dangerous constructions in order to reach the whole wall.

Two years of working alone however, began to make Nancy feel too isolated. She then turned to her second interest of art therapy, teaching photography to residents of a Richmond Fellowship House, a half-way post for ex-psychiatric patients. This she enjoyed very much.

Finally the idea came to her whereby she could bring together under one roof her different activities. It was to have her own studio, adapted for her needs, in which she could teach more classes, and do her own work. Once she believed she could make this dream become a reality, she set out very determinedly to set it up. To begin with she went round her locality, Walthamstow in East London, noting down all the empty properties, and then discovering who owned them, until at last she came upon a building owned by the local council but leased to a Housing Association who agreed to let Nancy take over the property on a no-rent-no-repairs basis. The building at that time needed a visionary approach to imagine that it ever could be usable, but Nancy obviously had that necessary gift and contacted GLAID (see Chapter 7, Grant giving Organisations) from whom she requested a grant for £200 for builders fees and materials, which was duly awarded. The Richmond Fellowship and the local authorities agreed to pay her to teach classes. She then arranged for workers from the Community Service Unit, (part of the Probation and After Care Service which deals with offenders who have been given Community Service Orders in lieu of prison sentences) to help do the necessary work, one of whom was a professional builder. An internal wall was knocked down to make a large, light room suitable for classes, and a second room is being transformed into Nancy's own studio. A loo and kitchen were also made usable.

At present Nancy has one weekly class, and one 'open day' a week and is getting together a third group to teach. Local people have discovered the studio and many have begun to come regularly to carry out their own artistic projects. She says that for the first time she has stopped wanting to go round the world, and is happy to have made a base for herself where she can work, and help other people who are attracted by the informal atmosphere she has created.

Rod Ward – Violin Maker

For those of you who, like me, always imagined that to make musical instruments you had to study and apprentice for hundreds of years, the story of Rod Ward will give you a pleasant surprise.

Rod is one of three craftsmen who have been installed to add a bit of 'rustic glamour' to a working farm which is open to the public. He seems happier to

93

make instruments than to give interviews to strange people such as myself, and parts of the talk were conducted by his six year old daughter who seemed to enjoy the whole affair much more, cleverly removing her father from the scene by announcing that the goat had escaped again, and proceeding to give a beautiful demonstration of his most complicated tools.

I did manage to learn however, that Rod's love of violins had been lifelong. He had first come to Riverside Farm to play his fiddle in the evenings. A wandering musician when he decided to try his hand at making a violin, he simply aimed to reproduce exactly the one he already had, using books to fill in the knowledge that he lacked. His very first instrument played, and was sold.

He then collected together his tools, books and materials, and with the farmer's blessing, converted at barn at the Farm into a workshop where he now makes violins and violas as a full-time occupation.

Selling the finished articles has never been a problem as there is always a demand for custom-made musical instruments. Rod could sell far more than he can make. He is now a member of the Devonshire Guild of Craftsmen, and is well known locally.

A. P. Woolrich – Model Maker

In the late summer of 1969, a strange virus resulting in sickness and giddiness, was the first sign of a course of events that was to lead to A. P. Woolrich completely changing his style of life.

Wrongly diagnosed as a temporary condition called Labinthitis, the illness forced him to take tranquillisers in order to cope with the symptoms. Eventually the tranquillisers affected his ability at work so much that he was asked to leave his job as an Assistant Work Study Engineer.

As travelling seemed to be one of the main factors aggravating his condition, he found a job in a local school to which he could walk every day.

Here he worked happily for a year until pressures began to build up, resulting in renewed attacks of dizziness and nausea, which were then correctly diagnosed as a permanent condition called Meniere's Disease. As the disease is not considered cureable, Mr Woolrich was retired by the school doctor as an insurance risk.

A light clerical job in an office was suggested, but, now a registered disabled person, he decided he was not willing to tolerate the resentment and lack of flexibility he believed he would have to suffer if he continued to work in open industry. Consequently he decided to work for himself. He and his wife made out a balance sheet of their skills and interest, their material assets and their liabilities. The final conclusion reached was that they could open a shop, or do some kind of craft work. They chose the latter.

In the past Mr Woolrich had served an engineering apprenticeship, with an additional five years as a journeyman. Also he had five years experience in Work Study, and so had an insight into modern methods and planning. He

94

also had a life-long interest in industrial history and in archaeology, subjects upon which he had built a good library of information. As a field of work which comprised all these skills and interests, he decided to build up a business making models of early industrial machinery and plant, for teaching purposes, museums and exhibitions. To supplement his income from this he was also prepared to tackle any light engineering work which would fit his workshop and machines.

Using his house as security, he was able to secure a bank loan of £2,500 to buy the tools and equipment needed. After a 2 ½ year search he found a smaller house with better workshop facilities and consequently sold his own house. The surplus from the sale allowed him to repay the bank loan. He applied to the local council for permission to work at home, which was granted, partly because he is disabled, and partly because he had no near neighbours to be irritated by any noise.

In the first days of the business, a problem arose with the earnings restrictions imposed upon people who receive Supplementary Benefit, which allows one to earn only a small amount before the Benefit is withdrawn. However, after a battle, he was given a weekly top-up payment so that their income never dropped below the basic flat-rate Supplementary Benefit payment. As soon as his income became at all regular however, all benefits were stopped. Being a low wage earner, but in full-time employment, he was awarded the Family Income Supplement which was a 'Godsend'. Gradually work began to build up. First orders included 17,000 little steel pins for the Local Authorities and, in the summer of 1973, a commission to make a pair of models of early blast furnaces dated about 1800. When these were completed and photographed, he had a concrete example of his work to show other potential customers.

Since making the workshop space in their new house fit to work in, their income has risen considerably. At the time of contacting me in 1977, he had £2,000 worth of orders on hand, and more 'feelers' going out.

He feels now that if he fails, it will not be through lack of demand for his work. Although the onset of his disability, and the many problems which have arisen during the setting up of the business have, at times, made life very difficult, the reward has been that he has been able to amalgamate his work with his hobby.

John Flack – Electraid Systems

John Flack had a road accident at the age of eleven which left him paralysed from the waist down. He was educated at the Lord Mayor Treloar College for handicapped boys where, in addition to a good academic training, he learnt a little about electrical engineering.

On leaving school he was unable to find a job, so he set about creating his own part-time work repairing radios.

In 1964 he started his first job as a production wireman with the Polio

Research Fund at Stoke Mandeville Hospital. The research team, whose aims were to develop electronic aids for the disabled, moved out of the hospital in 1969 to their own premises near Aylesbury, forming the company 'Possum Controls Limited'. For various reasons John felt that his future was not with this firm, and in November of the same year he left without any concrete ideas as to what to do next.

His first move however, was to establish 'Electraid' as a Company, which he did in 1970 without any ideas as to what product he could make or sell. His main drawback at the time was a lack of technical knowledge. Electronics is a rapidly changing field, and at Possums he was involved in fairly out-dated technology. His first priority therefore, was to familiarise himself with the latest components and design techniques, which he could then use to make a more effective product.

At the same time he worked on advance publicity by advertising 'Electraid' in Medical and Social Service Publications, both in this country and abroad. He was advertising an environmental control-system for £320, working at home on the design even though, at the time, he had not actually made one. He said this approach was absolutely necessary if he were to get anywhere at all.

His first customer was a lady with Multiple Sclerosis, via the Hertfordshire Social Services Department, who needed a typewriter controller. John adapted the design of his environmental control system to suit her needs. Six months later, a second order arrived for a special typewriter control, and at this point he decided to concentrate on developing controls for typewriters, and to abandon the environmental controls. From then on orders started to roll in every few months.

In 1973 he moved to his present premises in Aylesbury, a small prefabricated building, giving him space for a workshop with a lathe, drilling machine, and a small band-saw. He now employs two full time engineers, 2-3 part time helpers, and three women who carry out the production wiring in their own homes.

John sees expansion as inevitable, as there is a growing demand for his product which now enjoys an established reputation for being a versatile typewriter control system especially suitable for schools for the handicapped where one typewriter has to be used by a number of people with different disabilities. He has a long list of orders, mainly from the local Education Authorities, the Department of Employment, and various charities such as the Spastics Society.

As with many small businesses, cash-flow is still a problem. After having built and delivered a unit, it may be several months before he is paid. In the meantime he has to make overtures to his bank-manager whilst his account is overdrawn, and delay paying for the components used for as long as possible. In spite of this he has never had any serious debts, and is pleased that all through his life he has managed without claiming any financial assistance from the Government.

John is clearly dedicated to his venture, not only in the help he is giving to so many disabled people through his product, particularly by providing the means for severely handicapped children to communicate, but also by being an example of his strong belief that handicapped people should be able to do their own thing just like anybody else.

Paul Stone – Watch and Clock Repair

From his childhood Paul had watched and helped his grandfather at work in his profession of watch and clock repairing. It seemed natural for him to progress from school to Hackney Technical College where he studied horology.

At the college were students from all over the world who had come to study and to sit for the examinations designed by the British Horological Institute. For this course no real qualifications are needed, but students with some experience in the trade are favoured.

Paul started work in a small shop in Mere where he used to sit in the shop window and allow passers-by to watch him at work.

At the end of 1975 an opportunity presented itself to rent a little shop of his own where he is now happily installed.

His speciality is the repair of antique clocks. At the back of the shop is a tiny work-space where some machinery enables him to make up afresh the parts for clocks which have been too damaged to use again.

His passion for clocks carries over to his spare time when he devotes himself to making a copy of an antique clock with a self-winding mechanism that consists of a table which is tilted this way and that by the rolling of a heavy ball-bearing along a series of channels. The original of this clock is in the British Museum, and Paul hopes that, once completed, it will fetch a handsome price – a contribution towards a comfortable old-age.

Other successful projects

It is impossible to give examples of each of the ideas some imaginative person has turned into a means of earning a living, nor is this the purpose of the book, as the scope of ideas is limitless, and must depend to a large degree on the individual talents, skills and aspirations of whoever begins to plan his or her future along these lines.

However, to arm you with an antidote when gloomy people start hurling their prophesies of doom at you, saying 'Create your own work!? It can't be done!', here, to add to the projects previously outlined, is a further list of projects which are functioning successfully at the time of writing this book:-

Off-set Litho Printing; Silk-Screen Printing; machine knitting; translating; typesetting; making clothes for market stalls; making clothes for children; teaching at home; antique rug restoration; antique ivory restoration; rabbit farming; making leather brief cases; making military figures; making bellows; rush-work, including repairing rush cane-seats; carving wooden fireplaces;

97

heraldic sculpture; hand-carved wooden rocking horses and other wooden toys; making jackets and ponchos from woollen blankets; making pewter tableware; making acoustic guitars; making ornamental ironwork; making and designing in stained glass; cabinet making; making children's furniture; hand-made skin care products, and making wooden jig-saw puzzles.

CONCLUSION

It is difficult to draw conclusions from research which barely scratches the surface of such a complex subject as the creation of one's own work. However, a few generalisations can be made about the people and projects which are described in this book.

I expected to find that the people I met would have more in common than they actually did, but the two main features seem to run like a thread through a row of beads, are the persistence of the people concerned, and the unusual fact that they all enjoyed their work!

Persistance, compared to brilliance, or experience, or any other personality attribute, is undoubtedly the vital factor which must be possessed in order to work towards far-off goals despite the difficulties, bureaucratic stumbling blocks and set-backs which are almost inevitable. A positive attitude towards mistakes helps a great deal, as does a willingness and keenness to work hard, but the basic factor which separates the 'successful' from the 'failure' is that the successful just did not give up, whilst the so-called 'failure' were most likely potential successes who did not keep going long enough to realise it.

One of the reasons for this is possibly the idea we somehow have installed in us at school – the idea that when you leave school, particularly if you can flourish a handful of GCE Certificates, or better still a degree, at your prospective employers, you will almost immediately be earning as, if not more, than your parents, and will consequently be able to afford a car, a flat, lots of new clothes, holidays and all the other 'rights' of our materialistic society. Maybe this is the 'blackmail' needed to persuade lively teenagers to study boring lessons, but it leads to a false sense of instant success and instant reward.

Whatever the cause, lack of persistence seems to be synonymous with lack of confidence, and can to a large extent be alleviated by other people with their support and encouragement in times of low spirits. The 'I told-you-so' attitude has no place if we are to regain our confidence as creative individuals.

With regard to the people enjoying their work so much, this could be the result of a very careful choice of the type of work chosen, or a result of the style of working – the sense of achievement from using a whole variety of one's own resources on a scale small enough to retain one's sense of identity – but for whichever reason, the result was always a person who spoke proudly and enthusiastically about his work, his struggles and his plans for the future.

Finally, let us hope that government legislation will soon be geared to helping the self-employed and small businesses by simplifying the tedious paper-work which is still an unavoidable and time-consuming chore for all such people. Surely more help should be given to people who are trying to help themselves in real terms, rather than paying lip-service to self-help whilst

99

simultaneously piling up desks with clerical work which detracts, confuses and generally puts people off turning their creative ideas into reality.

At the moment society seems to exclude too many people from what must be a fundamental urge – to work productively – whilst at the same time openly rewarding those who are not excluded by financial payment, acceptance as 'useful' members of society, approval, prestige and esteem. It seems right and exciting to find the 'excluded' demanding their inclusion by carving out for themselves a place in which they can comfortably fit, live and work without compromise. Despite their difficulties these people leave you feeling that they have discovered the answer to a secret for which many others are still searching.

USEFUL ADDRESSES

Tim Appleyard (supplier of glass for engravers), 'Keepers', Church Lane, Bury, Nr Pulborough, Sussex.

The British Horological Institute, Upton Hall, Newark, Notts.

British Overseas Trade Board, 1 Victoria Street, London SW1.

Central Office of Information, Hercules Road, London SE1 7DU.

The Charity Commission, 14 Ryder Street, London.

The Chartered Institute of Patent Agents, Staple Inn Buildings, London WC1.

City Link Transport Services Limited, Kings Cross Freight Terminal, York Way, London N1.

Companies Registration Office, Crown Way, Maindy, Cardiff CF4 3UZ.

Cordwainers Technical College, Mare Street, London E8.

CoSIRA, (Reg Office) Queens House, Fish Row, Salisbury, Wilts SP1 1EX. (Information services) 35 Camp Road, Wimbledon, London SW19.

Crafts Advisory Committee (CAC), 12 Waterloo Place, London SW1.

The Design Centre, 28 Haymarket, London SW1.

The Embroiderer's Guild, 73 Wimpole Street, London W1.

Enterprise North, Co-Ordinating Centre, DUBS, Mill Hill Lane, Durham DH1 3LB.

The Facility of Astrological Studies, Hook Cottage, Vine Cross, Heathfield, Sussex.

The Federation of Working Communities, 5 Dryden Street, Covent Garden, London WC0 9NW.

Finance for Industry (FFI), 7 Copthall Avenue, London EC2R 7DD.

Forum of Private Business Ltd, Ruskin Rooms, Drury Lane, Knutsford, Cheshire WA16 0ED.

The Franchise Advisory Centre, 32 Stockwell Park Crescent, London SW9.

GLAID, Flat 4, 188 Ramsden Road, Balham, SW12.

The Glasshouse, 27 Neal Street, London WC2.

HM Patent Office (Department of Trade and Industry), Southampton Buildings, Chancery Lane, London WC2.

HIDB, Bridge House, 27 Bank Street, Inverness, Scotland.

ICOM, Beechwood College, Elmer Lane, Leeds.

ICOF, 1 Gold Street, Northampton NN1 1SA.

Jewellery Summer School, Mill Wynd, Lundin Links, Fyfe, Scotland.

Joint Crafts Committee (JCC), Scottish Economic Planning Department, St Andrew's House, Edinburgh, Scotland.

LEDU, 21 Linehall Street, Belfast 2, Northern Ireland.

LEP Packing Limited, Corney Road, London W4.

London College of Furniture & Musical Technology, 41-47 Commercial Road, London E1.

101

London Enterprise Agency, 69 Cannon Street, London EC4N 5AB.

Mantor Export Services 26 Hockerill Street, Bishops Stortford, Herts

The National Federation of Women's Institutes, 39 Eccleston Street, London SW1W 9NT.

National Research and Development Corporation, Kingsgate House, 66-74 Victoria St, London SW1E 6SL.

PIRA, Randalls Road, Leatherhead, Surrey.

Pitt & Scott Limited, Packers, 20 Eden Grove, London N7.

Possum Users Association, 'Copper Beech', Parry's Close, Stoke Bishops, Bristol BS9 1AW.

Post Office Information Service – 01.606 9876.

The Preparatory Training Bureau, RADAR, 25 Mortimer Street, London W1N 8AB.

Regional Development Grants Division, Department of Industry, Millbank, SW1.

Road Haulage Association, 22 Upper Woburn Place, London WC1.

St Nicholas Training Centre for Montessori Method of Education, 22 Princes Gate, London SW7.

Scottish Council (Development and Industry), 1 Castle Street, Edinburgh EH2 3AJ.

Scottish Design Centre, 72 Vincent Street, Glasgow, C2.

Scottish Development Agency, 102 Telford Road, Edinburgh EH4 2NP.

SICRAS, 27 Walker Street, Edinburgh, Scotland.

The Welsh Development Agency, Small Business Division, Treforest Industrial Estate, Pontypridd, CF37 5UT, Mid Glams.

Useful Publications

ADVERTISERS ANNUAL – Business Publications Limited, (at Reference Libraries).

ARTS REVIEW YEARBOOK AND DIRECTORY – Richard Gainsborough Periodicals Limited, 8 Wyndham Place, London W1.

A COMPREHENSIVE GUIDE TO TOWN PLANNING LAW AND PROCEDURES, Robert McBrown, Published by George Godwin.

COURSES LEADING TO THE DIPLOMA IN ART AND DESIGN – The Art and Design Admissions Registry, 16 Albian Place, Maidstone, Kent.

THE CRAFT BUSINESS – Rosemary Petit, Pitman Publishing Limited, Pitman House, 39 Parker Street, London WC2B 5BP.

CRAFT WORKSHOPS IN THE COUNTRYSIDE – CoSIRA, 35 Camp Road, Wimbledon SW19.

CRAFTS – The Crafts Advisory Committee, 12 Waterloo Place, London SW1.

DESIGN – The Design Centre, 28 Haymarket, London SW1.

DIRECTORY OF DESIGN COURSES IN THE UK – The Design Council, 18 Haymarket, SW1.

THE DIRECTORY OF FURTHER EDUCATION – Hobons Press (Cambridge) Ltd, (at Reference Libraries).

DIRECTORY OF GRANT MAKING TRUSTS – The Charities Aid Fund, National Council of Social Service, 26 Bedford Square, London WC1. (at Reference Libraries).

EXPORT HANDBOOK – British Overseas Trade Board, 1 Victoria Street, London SW1.

EXPORT MADE EASY – CoSIRA, 35 Camp Road, Wimbledon SW19.

FLOODLIGHT – The Inner London Education Authority (Newsagents).

IN THE MAKING — 'Acorn', 34 Church Street, Wolverton, Milton Keynes, Bucks.

INCORPORATION OF NEW COMPANIES? NOTES FOR GUIDANCE, and NOTES FOR THE GUIDANCE OF REGISTERED COMPANIES, Companies Registration Office, Crown Way, Maindy, Cardiff, CF4 3UZ.

KOMPASS – Kompass Publications Limited, Stuart House, 41-43 Perrymount Road, Haywards Heath, Sussex.

MARKETS YEAR BOOK – World's Fair Limited, Union Street, Oldham. (at Reference Libraries).

MUSEUMS AND GALLERIES IN GREAT BRITAIN AND IRELAND, ABC Travel Guides Limited, Oldhill, Dunstable, Bedford.

THE PROFESSIONAL PRACTICE OF DESIGN – Dorothy Goslett, B T Batsford Limited, 4 Fitzhardinge Street, London W1.

RURAL RESETTLEMENT HANDBOOK – Dick Kitto, The Manor, Thelneatham, Nr Diss, Norfolk.

SO YOU WANT TO START A FACTORY? – from local Factory Inspectorate.
UHURU – A WORKING ALTERNATIVE – Uhuru, 53 Cowley Road, Oxford.
WHERE – Advisory Centre for Education, 32 Trumpington Street, Cambridge.
THE YEAR BOOK OF ADULT EDUCATION – National Institute of Adult Education, 35 Queen Anne Street, London W1, and/or The Scottish Institute of Adult Education, 57 Melville Street, Edinburgh.